VISIONARY LEADERSHIP
in Healthcare

Excellence in Practice, Policy, and Ethics

Holly Wei, PhD, RN, NEA-BC, FAAN
Sara Horton-Deutsch, PhD, RN, PMHCNS, FAAN, ANEF

Sigma
GLOBAL NURSING
EXCELLENCE

Sigma Theta Tau International Honor Society of Nursing (Sigma) is a nonprofit organization whose mission is developing nurse leaders anywhere to improve healthcare everywhere. Founded in 1922, Sigma has more than 135,000 active members in over 100 countries and territories. Members include practicing nurses, instructors, researchers, policymakers, entrepreneurs, and others. Sigma's more than 540 chapters are located at more than 700 institutions of higher education throughout Armenia, Australia, Botswana, Brazil, Canada, Colombia, Croatia, England, Eswatini, Ghana, Hong Kong, Ireland, Israel, Italy, Jamaica, Japan, Jordan, Kenya, Lebanon, Malawi, Mexico, the Netherlands, Nigeria, Pakistan, Philippines, Portugal, Puerto Rico, Scotland, Singapore, South Africa, South Korea, Sweden, Taiwan, Tanzania, Thailand, the United States, and Wales. Learn more at www.sigmanursing.org.

Sigma Theta Tau International
550 West North Street
Indianapolis, IN, USA 46202

To request a review copy for course adoption, order additional books, buy in bulk, or purchase for corporate use, contact Sigma Marketplace at 888.654.4968 (US/Canada toll-free), +1.317.687.2256 (International), or solutions@sigmamarketplace.org.

To request author information, or for speaker or other media requests, contact Sigma Marketing at 888.634.7575 (US/Canada toll-free) or +1.317.634.8171 (International).

ISBN: 9781646480616
PDF ISBN: 9781646480623

First Printing, 2022

Publisher: Dustin Sullivan
Acquisitions Editor: Emily Hatch
Development Editor: Jill Stanley
Cover Designer: Michael Tanamachi
Interior Design/Page Layout: Rebecca Batchelor

Managing Editor: Carla Hall
Publications Specialist: Todd Lothery
Project Editor: Jill Stanley
Copy Editor: Erin Geile
Proofreader: Todd Lothery

ABOUT THE LEAD AUTHORS

Holly Wei, PhD, RN, NEA-BC, FAAN, is a Professor and Assistant Dean for the PhD program at the University of Louisville School of Nursing. Her overarching research focuses on healthcare organizational culture, leadership development, clinician well-being, stress genomic biomarkers, and patient care quality. She is known nationally and internationally for her nursing practice models and a Convergent Care Theory. Multiple healthcare systems have used Wei's nursing models to guide practice and promote organizational culture and patient care with significant improvements in nursing practice and patient care quality.

Wei's scholarly work has reached and influenced the nursing profession in academia and clinical nursing practice globally. In the past five years, Wei had 50 peer-reviewed publications and delivered over 70 presentations, including radio and TV interviews, influencing tens of thousands of nurses globally. Some of her articles are within the top-read, top-downloaded, and top-cited articles of journals. Wei is an Associate Editor of the *International Journal for Human Caring.* She sits on two boards of directors and two journals' editorial board positions, including *Advances in Nursing Science.*

Wei has received numerous prestigious awards throughout her career. Recently, she received the International Leininger Caring-Culture Award, Board of Governors Distinguished Professor for Teaching, DAISY Extraordinary Faculty, Nurse Educator of the Year, Scholar-Teacher Award, Outstanding Research Scholar Award, and Nursing Research Award. These awards affirm her significant contributions and influences in nursing leadership and practice regionally and globally.

Sara Horton-Deutsch, PhD, RN, PMHCNS, FAAN, ANEF, is a Caritas Coach and a Professor and the Director of the Kaiser Permanente/USF Partnership at the University of San Francisco, where she mentors the next generation of nursing leaders through the lens of Caring Science and values-based leadership. She also serves as a Faculty Associate with the Watson Caring Science Institute. In 2021, she co-created and initiated the Caritas Leadership Program, a uniquely customized six-month program guiding participants through executive Caring Science leader dialogues, interactive circles, and participant transformation projects. She is also a founding partner of Better Together Healing, LLC, a holistic practice partnership specializing in an integrative approach to heal the self, build collaborations, and create healthy and bounded communities. As a therapeutic practitioner and Caritas leadership coach, she collaborates with healthcare professionals and organizations seeking balance and growth who are open to engaging in innovative approaches to healing. Her comprehensive approach includes certifications in professional coaching and training through the Leadership Circle and Working with Resilience, providing comprehensive profiles and assessments to raise the conscious practice of leadership and build regenerative success at work.

Horton-Deutsch holds a research fellowship at the University of South Africa School of Human Sciences, where she encourages critical discourse and collaborates with faculty to enhance research and scholarship. Her research foci are on leadership development, reflective practice, and creating healing and healthy work environments. She has co-edited four textbooks. Her work has been published in three books with Sigma: *Reflective Practice: Transforming Education and Improving Outcomes* (2012 & 2017), *Reflective Organizations: On the Front Lines of QSEN & Reflective Practice Implementation* (2015), and *Caritas Coaching: A Journey Toward Transpersonal Caring for Informed Moral Action in Healthcare* (2018).

Her most recent awards, honors, and fellowships include 2020–2021 Experienced Academic Nurse Leadership Academy Faculty Mentor, Sigma; 2018–2019 Faculty Fellowship in Ignatian Tradition, University of San Francisco; 2016–2024 Invited Research Fellow, University of South Africa, Johannesburg, South Africa; 2016–2017 Nurse Faculty Leadership Academy, Faculty Mentor, Sigma; 2014 Fellow, American Academy of Nursing; 2013 Fellow, Academy of Nursing Education; Fellow, National League for Nursing.

CONTRIBUTING AUTHORS

(For expanded bios, see this book's page on the Sigma Repository: http://hdl.handle.net/10755/22206)

Stephanie Wilkie Ahmed, DNP, NP-BC, is Associate Chief Nursing Officer and Watson Caring Science Scholar in Residence in the University of Miami Health System.

Mary Jo Assi, DNP, RN, NEA-BC, FAAN, is Associate Chief Nursing Officer and Partner, Strategic Consulting, at Press Ganey.

Nancy M. Ballard, PhD, RN, NEA-BC, is Assistant Professor at Kennesaw State University.

Mark D. Beck, DNP, MSN, BS, RN, is Assistant Professor and Interim Program Director at Samuel Merritt University.

Wanda J. Borges, PhD, RN, ANP-BC, is Dean and Professor, and Associate Director of Graduate Programs in the School of Nursing at New Mexico State University.

Sylvia T. Brown, EdD, RN, CNE, ANEF, is Dean and Professor at the East Carolina University College of Nursing.

Chantal Cara, PhD, RN, FAAN, FCAN, is Professor at Université de Montréal and a Distinguished Caring Science Scholar at the Watson Caring Science Institute.

Laura Caramanica, PhD, RN, CNE, CNEP, FACHE, FAAN, is Graduate Program Director and Professor at the University of West Georgia.

Gabrielle Dawn Childs, MA, MPH, RN, is a PhD Candidate at the American Graduate School in Paris and a Program Manager for the Peace Corps' Advancing Health Professionals program.

Peggy L. Chinn, PhD, DSc(Hon), RN, FAAN, is the Editor of the journal *Advances in Nursing Science* and Professor Emerita at the University of Connecticut.

Carey S. Clark, PhD, RN, AHN-BSC RYT, FAAN, is Professor and Director of Nursing at Pacific College of Health and Science.

Jim D'Alfonso, DNP, PhD(h), RN, NEA-BC, FNAP, FAAN, is Executive Director, Professional Excellence and the KP Scholars Academy, & Adjunct Faculty at the University of San Francisco.

Erica DeKruyter, MSN, RN, is Manager of Educational Resources at Sigma Theta Tau International Honor Society of Nursing (Sigma).

Jennifer J. Doering, PhD, RN, is Associate Dean for Academic Affairs and Associate Professor at the University of Wisconsin-Milwaukee College of Nursing.

Diana Drake, DNP, APRN, WHNP, FAAN, FNAP, is Clinical Professor and Director of the Women's Health Gender-Related Nurse Practitioner specialty at the University of Minnesota School of Nursing.

Karen J. Foli, PhD, RN, FAAN, is Associate Professor in the Purdue University School of Nursing.

Lynn Gallagher-Ford, PhD, RN, NE-BC, DPFNAP, FAAN/Evidence-based Practice (CH), is Chief Operating Officer and Director of the Helene Fuld National Trust Institute for Evidence-based Practice in Nursing and Healthcare at the Ohio State University College of Nursing.

Stephanie D. Gingerich, DNP, RN, CPN, is Clinical Assistant Professor at the University of Minnesota School of Nursing.

Kaboni Whitney Gondwe, PhD, RN, is Assistant Professor at the University of Wisconsin-Milwaukee College of Nursing.

Ernest J. Grant, PhD, RN, FAAN, is President of the American Nurses Association.

Sarah E. Gray, DNP, RN, CEN, FAEN, is Chief Nursing Officer for Sigma Theta Tau International Honor Society of Nursing (Sigma).

Christine Griffin, PhD, RN, NPD-BC, CPN, is a Caritas Coach and Professional Development Specialist at Children's Hospital Colorado.

Senem Guney, PhD, is Vice President of Language Analytics for Press Ganey.

Sonya R. Hardin, PhD, CCRN, NP-C, FAAN, is Dean and Professor at the University of Louisville.

Grissel Hernandez, PhD, RN, MPH, HNB-BC, NPD-BC, SGAHN, is Executive Director at Stanford Health Care's Center for Education and Professional Development.

Marcia Hills, PhD, RN, FAAN, CFAN, is Professor and Associate Director of Research and Scholarship at the University of Victoria's School of Nursing.

Phyllis N. Horns, PhD, RN, FAAN, is Professor of Nursing and Director of the East Carolina Consortium for Nursing Leadership at the East Carolina University College of Nursing.

Matthew S. Howard, DNP, RN, CEN, TCRN, CPEN, CPN, is Director of Scholarship and Leadership Resources at Sigma Theta Tau International Honor Society of Nursing (Sigma).

Rachel Johnson-Koenke, PhD, LCSW, is Assistant Professor at the University of Colorado College of Nursing.

Christie Kerwan, MSN, RN, is Director of Strategic Partnerships—Healthcare for PowerDMS.

Judy Ngele Khanyola, MSc, BSN, RN, is Chair for the Center for Nursing and Midwifery at the University of Global Health Equity in Rwanda.

Carol Ann King, DNP, MSN, BSN, RN, FNP-BC, NHDP-BC, is Clinical Professor in the Doctor of Nursing Practice–Family and Adult-Gerontology Nurse Practitioner programs at East Carolina University.

Dame Donna Kinnair, MA, RGN, HV, LLB, PGCE, is Chief Executive and General Secretary of the Royal College of Nursing in the UK.

Wipada Kunaviktikul, PhD, RN, RM, FAAN, is Professor Emerita and Assistant to the President of Health Science Academic Affairs at Panyapiwat Institute of Management in Thailand.

Donna Lake, PhD, RN, NEA-BC, FAAN, is Clinical Professor at the East Carolina University College of Nursing.

Jeneile Luebke PhD, RN, is a post-doctoral Nurse Research Fellow at the University of Wisconsin-Madison.

Elizabeth A. Madigan, PhD, RN, FAAN, is Chief Executive Officer of Sigma Theta Tau International Honor Society of Nursing (Sigma).

Kathy Malloch, PhD, MBA, RN, FAAN, is Clinical Professor at the Ohio State University College of Nursing.

Lucy Mkandawire-Valhmu, PhD, RN, is Associate Professor at the University of Wisconsin-Milwaukee College of Nursing.

Chelsie Monroe, MSN, APRN, PMHNP-BC, is a Psychiatric Mental Health Nurse Practitioner and Owner of Balanced Mental Wellness in Colorado.

Melissa T. Ojemeni, PhD, RN, is Director of Nursing Education, Research and Professional Development for Partners In Health in Boston.

Crystal Oldman, EdD, MSc, MA, RN, RHV, QN, FRCN, CBE, is Chief Executive at the Queen's Nursing Institute in the UK.

Danielle EK Perkins, PhD, RN, is the former Manager of the Center for Excellence in Nursing Education at Sigma Theta Tau International Honor Society of Nursing (Sigma).

Daniel J. Pesut, PhD, RN, FAAN, is Emeritus Professor at the University of Minnesota School of Nursing and Emeritus Katherine R. and C. Walton Lillehei Chair of Nursing Leadership at the University of Minnesota.

Tim Porter-O'Grady, DM, EdD, ScD(h), APRN, FAAN, FACCWS, is Senior Partner for Tim Porter-O'Grady Associates LLC & Clinical Professor at the Emory University School of Nursing.

Teddie M. Potter, PhD, RN, FAAN, FNAP, is Clinical Professor, Director of Planetary Health, and Coordinator of the Doctor of Nursing Practice in Health Innovation and Leadership program at the University of Minnesota School of Nursing.

Katherine Reed, LPC, is Program Manager of the Ponzio Creative Arts Therapy program at Children's Hospital Colorado.

Jennifer Reese, MD, is Associate Professor of Clinical Pediatrics at the University of Colorado School of Medicine and Section Head of the Pediatric Hospital Medicine.

William E. Rosa, PhD, MBE, NP-BC, FAANP, FAAN, is Chief Research Fellow at Memorial Sloan Kettering Cancer Center's Department of Psychiatry and Behavioral Sciences.

Barbara Sattler, DrPH, RN, FAAN, is Professor Emerita at the University of San Francisco School of Nursing and Health Professions.

Gwen Sherwood, PhD, RN, FAAN, ANEF, is Professor Emerita at the University of North Carolina at Chapel Hill School of Nursing.

Michelle Taylor Skipper, DNP, FNP-BC, NHDP-BC, FAANP, is Director of the Adult-Gerontology and Family Nurse Practitioner specialties of the DNP program at the East Carolina University College of Nursing.

Chandra L. Speight, PhD, RN, NP-C, CNE, is Assistant Professor in the Department of Advanced Nursing Practice and Education at the East Carolina University College of Nursing.

Allison Squires, PhD, RN, FAAN, is Associate Professor and Director of the PhD program at the New York University Rory Meyers College of Nursing.

Dennis A. Taylor, DNP, PhD, ACNP-BC, NEA-BC, FCCM, is a Trauma Acute Care Nurse Practitioner and teaches in the Department of Academic Nursing at Wake Forest Baptist Health.

Todd E. Tussing, DNP, RN, CENP, NEA-BC, is Assistant Professor of Clinical Nursing at the Ohio State University College of Nursing.

Gisela H. van Rensburg is Professor at the University of South Africa.

AnnMarie Lee Walton, PhD, MPH, RN, OCN, CHES, FAAN, is Assistant Professor at the Duke University School of Nursing.

Kefang Wang, PhD, RN, FAAN, is Dean and Professor in the School of Nursing and Rehabilitation at Shandong University in China.

Jean Watson, PhD, RN, AHN-BC, HSGAHN, FAAN, LL (AAN), is Distinguished Professor and Founder/Director of the Watson Caring Science Institute in Colorado.

Ena M. Williams, MBA/MSM, RN, CENP, is Senior Vice President and Chief Nursing Officer at Yale New Haven Hospital.

Kenichi Yamaguchi, PhD, is Associate Professor at the Okinawa Prefectural College of Nursing in Japan.

TABLE OF CONTENTS

INTRODUCTION

This Facilitator Guide is designed to work with the textbook and Learner Activities Workbook and follows a similar format. It includes reflective questions and guiding answers, narratives and guiding responses, quizzes and answers, and PowerPoint slides. Learners can use the reflective questions and narratives to guide their reading, thinking, and group discussions or activities.

Like the textbook, this Facilitator Guide comprises five parts, which support nurse leaders' development in clinical practice or academic settings.

Below is a brief introduction of the five parts.

PART I

The guide presents leadership theories in organizations. There are four topics in this part, which are closely connected:

1. The evolution of leadership theories from ancient times to the present

2. Nursing as both discipline and profession shaped by the conditions and attributes of influential nurse leaders, historically relevant theoretical and philosophical perspectives, and paradigm shifts in healthcare

3. The influence of our knowledge of complex adaptive systems and the neuroscience of interactions on leadership development and implications for healthcare practices

4. Promotion of strengths-based leadership and positive leadership to help readers develop effective communication, conflict management, team building, and leadership skills

PART II

Leadership's roles in creating healthy work environments are addressed. The four topics in this part support readers in establishing and promoting organizational culture and environments:

1. Ways to nurture a healthy and healing environment

2. Leadership's roles in promoting a resilient healthcare workforce

3. Leadership's opportunities in mitigating organizational trauma and supportive strategies from a Caring Science perspective

4. The role of planetary and environmental health in leading and enhancing human-universe relationships

PART III

Four visionary leadership theories are applied in practice:

1. Quantum Leadership and ways to integrate it into healthcare

2. Using caring leadership and Caring Science to guide leadership practice

3. Organizational strategies to promote exceptional patient experience through Compassionate Connected Care®

4. The application of complexity theory to inform population and community health

PART IV

The role of nurse leadership in collaboration, leading change, and innovation is presented:

1. The importance of a unifying workforce to improve interprofessional collaboration and healthcare

2. Reinforcing leadership's roles in collaboration for disaster preparedness and response

3. The importance of collaboration and leading change at a global level

4. Promoting research, quality, and evidence-informed practice

PART V

The last part envisions the future of nurse leadership:

1. Defining wisdom leaders to inform personal and professional leadership development

2. Addressing diversity, equity, and inclusion (DEI) in academia and clinical settings, and specific strategies to support BIPOC (Black, Indigenous, and people of color) nurse scholars

3. Calling for nurses' and healthcare professionals' actions to advocate and get involved in policy change

4. Healthcare leadership in social and political determinants of health

5. Calling healthcare leaders to create a more connected world through an Ethic of Face and Belonging

With an emphasis on collaboration and partnerships, this book moves away from hierarchical forms of leadership to teach more engaged, open, equitable, inclusive, authentic, and caring leadership styles.

PRESENTATION STRATEGIES

HOW COULD/SHOULD THE SESSIONS BE ORGANIZED?

The guide comprises five parts/sections. Facilitators can guide students through the parts based on their course content and learning outcomes. If this is the leading textbook you use, you may go with the book sequence or change to a different order. The five parts of the book will take learners on a journey of leadership development in the following order: 1) Leadership theories in organizations; 2) The development and maintenance of healthy work environments; 3) Applying leadership theories in practice; 4) The role of nurse leadership in collaboration, leading change, and innovation; and 5) Envisioning the future of nurse leadership. Many nurses are on a vision quest standing in a gap between where they find themselves and transitioning from what they once were to whom they are becoming. Therefore, as a secondary text, focus on the sections of the book that emphasize the formation of the nurse leader and how they balance their doing with being and becoming to support this transformational process.

WHAT ARE THE COURSE OBJECTIVES, AND WHICH SECTIONS OF THE BOOK COVER EACH OBJECTIVE?

You may develop the course objectives based on your program needs. The following are some examples of course objectives:

- Assess organizational culture, climates, and policies to promote equity, inclusion, team engagement, and interprofessional collaborations in the healthcare system. Parts 1 & 2.

- Advocate for nursing practices that improve healthcare delivery and health policy outcomes. Parts 2 & 3.

- Integrate leadership theories in nursing practices to accelerate the transformation of healthcare through professional identify and engagement. Parts 3 & 4.

- Synthesize effective leadership strategies to manage ethical dilemmas inherent to social justice, equity, and ethical healthcare. Part 4.

- Analyze health policies to envision the future of nurse leadership. Parts 4 & 5.

WHAT IS MY ROLE AS A FACILITATOR?

As a facilitator, you encourage learners to read, reflect, discuss, and apply the leadership theories and skills learned throughout the semester. While there are many ways you can facilitate, here are a few examples for your reference:

1. Assign readings and encourage learners to read the assigned chapters ahead of the class meeting or, conversely, present a case and have the readers go to assigned readings to discover solutions.

2. Introduce course materials using PowerPoints.

3. Use reflective questions to encourage learners to discuss leadership or policy-related challenges learners face.

4. Assign essays where learners integrate their context and experience with reflections on course materials and current challenges.

5. Assess learners' knowledge using quizzes.

WHAT DELIVERY METHOD SHOULD I PLAN?

You can use lectures (we recommend limiting to short theory bursts), visual presentations, roundtable discussions, group activities, workshops, journaling, and seminars. The course materials can be delivered via traditional in-classroom instruction, online, and hybrid teaching (asynchronous and synchronous).

ARE OUTSIDE CLASSROOM ACTIVITIES ALSO SUGGESTED?

Learners may expand and deepen their learning via mentorship and hands-on experience. With that, you may add outside classroom activities, such as job shadowing, interviews, clinical application, and community service.

FACILITATOR RESOURCES

This guide provides facilitators with the following resources for each chapter:

- Reflective questions
- Narratives
- Quizzes
- PowerPoints

REFLECTIVE QUESTIONS

Each chapter typically contains five reflective questions. These questions are designed to prompt learners' reflection or discussion about the chapter content. Facilitators can use the reflective questions to help learners reflect on the materials read, shift their reflection from content to thought, and put learners at the center of the learning process. While the answers to the reflective questions vary, this guide provides facilitators with guiding solutions for reference.

NARRATIVES

Each chapter includes a narrative. A narrative is a way of telling true or fictitious events, representing a situation the chapter addresses. Facilitators can use the narratives to promote learners' discussion and understanding of the chapter content.

QUIZZES

There are typically 10 quiz questions in each chapter. The questions are a mix of multiple choice and true/false questions. Facilitators can use the quiz questions to evaluate learners' understanding at the end of teaching or use the quizzes as a pre-post teaching tool.

POWERPOINTS

PowerPoints are provided for each chapter. The slides highlight the significant points of the chapter. PowerPoints can be an effective tool for facilitators to present the chapter material in classrooms, improve visual effects, and encourage learning. Facilitators can modify the PowerPoints provided based on their needs, design their own slides, and use them for teaching. Access the PowerPoints via the link or QR code below.

https://www.sigmanursing.org/visionary-leadership-in-healthcare

SYLLABUS/COURSE CALENDAR

Institutions of higher learning have many different term lengths, but typically offer 8-, 12-, or 16-week terms. Providing a suggested syllabus or course calendar can be very useful for instructors using your guide. These can be just basic or general, but the more details the better. New instructors or instructors with little prep time will especially appreciate this kind of material. Consider providing for at least the three term lengths mentioned above.

Online courses are going to be organized into modules, which generally are covered either one per week or one for every two weeks, i.e., eight modules for an 8- or 16-week course, etc. Traditional courses are going to meet once or more per week, for whatever length of the term. Commonly, even traditional courses will have material that is required to be built in a learning management system, such as Canvas or Blackboard. Thus, providing a weekly or module-by-module course calendar will work for both course formats. Consider what is a reasonable workload per week in chunking up the material for the various term lengths.

A typical syllabus or course calendar guide for covering material with module reading recommendations per term length:

16-WEEK TERM (9 HRS/WEEK OR 18 HRS/MOD)	12-WEEK TERM (18 HRS/MOD)	8-WEEK TERM (16-17 HRS/MOD)
Weeks 1 & 2: Ch 1-3	Module 1: Ch 1-2	Module 1: Ch 1-2
Weeks 3 & 4: Ch 4-6	Module 2: Ch 3-4	Module 2: Ch 3-5
Weeks 5 & 6: Ch 7-9	Module 3: Ch 5-6	Module 3: Ch 6-10
Weeks 7 & 8: Ch 10-12	Module 4: Ch 7-8	Module 4: Ch 11-14
Weeks 9 & 10: Ch 13-15	Module 5: Ch 9-10	Module 5: Ch 15-17
Weeks 11 & 12: Ch 16-18	Module 6: Ch 11-12	Module 6: Ch 18-19
Weeks 13 & 14: Ch 19-20	Module 7: Ch 13-14	Module 7: Ch 20-21
Week 15: Ch 21	Module 8: Ch 15-16	Module 8: Review
Week 16: Review	Module 9: Ch 17-18	
	Module 10: Ch 19-20	
	Module 11: Ch 21	
	Module 12: Review	

Notice that the amount of "hours" for each term length is the same overall—all term lengths will cover the same amount of material.

RECOMMENDED EXAMPLES FOR MODULES IN A CMS/LMS

Whether delivered online or in a traditional format, most institutions use course management systems and expect the course to be at least partially built in the CMS/LMS. Thus, courses are usually built in "modules." A module can be as simple as just a list of assignments, but the most effective content presentation provides more. Below is a typical outline for a module build in a CMS/LMS.

Each module includes the following components:

1. Module introduction

2. Module objectives

3. Textbook reading assignments

4. Learning activities

5. Assessments

    a. Discussion board

    b. Quiz/Test item bank (should be provided)

    c. Paper

    d. Suggested topics

    e. Presentation

    f. Group work

6. Module summary including review of objectives

7. Faculty guidelines for grading each assessment per module

A generic sample module covering the topic "Introduction to Health Policy and Evidence-Informed Policymaking" (excerpted from the Facilitator Guide for *Evidence-Informed Health Policy* and provided here only as guidance for structure, not content) is provided below.

GENERIC SAMPLE MODULE

INTRODUCTION

In this module, the use of evidence in policymaking will be introduced, particularly in terms of adapted EBP models for use in health policy. Evidence-informed policymaking will be described. Sources for guiding the evaluation of evidence and the evidence hierarchy will be reviewed. Strategies for using evidence in policymaking will be explored. Lastly, health policy as both an entity and a process will be investigated.

MODULE OBJECTIVES

1. Describe the use of evidence in health policymaking.

2. Compare and contrast evidence-based and evidence-informed policymaking.

3. Explain how hierarchical evidence can be used in policymaking.

4. Identify key sources that can be used to guide the evaluation of evidence.

5. Examine how health policy can be both a process and an entity.

6. Differentiate between the big P and the little p in health policy.

MODULE READING ASSIGNMENT

Read Chapters 1, 2, and 3 from the text: Loversidge, J. M., & Zurmehly, J. (2019). *Evidence-informed health policy: Using EBP to transform policy in nursing and healthcare.* Indianapolis, IN: Sigma Theta Tau International. These readings are related to module objectives (MO) 1–6.

MODULE LEARNING ACTIVITIES

Read Chapter 1 from the text. Pay particular attention to the definitions of evidence-informed policymaking including the essential elements and the various EBP models and evidence-informed health policy models and their potential use in policymaking. This reading relates to MO 1 and 2.

Read Chapter 2 from the text. Pay particular attention to how evidence can be used and the levels of the evidence-based medicine pyramid. This reading relates to MO 3 and 4.

Read Chapter 3 from the text. These readings are related to MO 5 and 6.

Access and explore the Centers for Disease Control and Prevention [CDC] Policy Process at https://www.cdc.gov/policy/analysis/process/index.html. Pay particular attention to the policy process as outlined in Figure 1. This activity relates to MO 5.

Watch the brief (less than 5–10 minute) faculty-developed YouTube video: "Module 1 Overview: Introduction to health policy and evidence-informed policymaking." (YouTube is recommended as it provides closed captioning for accessibility.) This activity relates to MO 1–6.

Check announcements for news of current events in health policy. This activity relates to MO 1.

Complete the designated assessment. The completion of the designated assessment relates to MO 1–6. See the specific assessment item for module outcome relationship.

ASSESSMENTS

Pick and choose from the various options below.

SAMPLE DISCUSSION BOARD ITEMS (CHOOSE FROM AMONG THESE)

1. Compare and contrast the four definitions of evidence-informed health policymaking as presented in your text: Ball, 2018; Loversidge, 2016; Oxman, et al., 2009; and World Health Organization, 2018. (From Student Workbook [SW] page 10.) This activity relates to MO 1.

2. Discuss the rationale for using the term *informed* versus *based* when applying evidence to policymaking, using the definitions as your source documents. (From SW page 11.) This activity relates to MO 2.

3. Describe the various levels of the EBM pyramid and provide one example of the use of hierarchical evidence in policymaking. This activity relates to MO 3.

4. Identify at least two key sources that are helpful in guiding users to evaluate evidence and provide at least one example of how at least one of sources has been used in evidence evaluation. This activity relates to MO 4.

5. Compare and contrast health policy as an entity or a process by identifying key elements or keywords. (From SW page 14.) This activity relates to MO 5.

6. Differentiate between big P health policy and little p health policy and provide an example of each (from SW page 15). This activity relates to MO 6.

PAPER

Brief annotated bibliography in table format specific to a student-identified health policy problem.

LEARNING ACTIVITY

Assign the learning activity in the SW on page 12 and 13. The student must include a minimum of four articles. This activity relates to MO 3.

QUIZ—CHOOSE FROM THESE:

1. Create a quiz focused on differentiation between policy as an entity and policy as a process. The activity on page 14 of the SW can serve as the foundation for this quiz. This would be a 10-item matching quiz. Match each statement to either entity or process. This activity relates to MO 5.

2. Create a quiz focused on distinguishing among government policy, nongovernment policy, and policy at the intersection of the two. The activity on page 15 of the SW can serve as the foundation for developing this quiz. This would be a 12-item matching quiz. Match each statement to big P, little p, or intersection Pp. This activity relates to MO 6.

3. Create a two-item quiz by combining 1 and 2. This activity relates to MO 5 & 6.

MODULE SUMMARY

In this module, the use of evidence in policymaking was introduced, particularly in terms of adapted EBP models for use in health policy. Evidence-informed policymaking was described, and examples provided. Various sources for guiding the evaluation of evidence as well as the evidence-based medicine hierarchy were reviewed. Strategies for using evidence in policymaking were discussed. Lastly, health policy as both an entity and a process was explored.

FACULTY GUIDELINES FOR GRADING MODULE

SAMPLE DISCUSSION BOARD ITEMS (CHOOSE FROM THESE)

1. Compare and contrast the four definitions of evidence-informed health policymaking as presented in your text: Ball, 2018; Loversidge, 2016; Oxman, et al., 2009; and World Health Organization, 2018 (From SW page 10. The answer is provided on page 23 of the Instructor's Guide [IG]).

2. Discuss the rationale for using the term *informed* versus *based* when applying evidence to policymaking, using the definitions as your source documents. (This item is from SW page 11.) Guidelines for the instructor response can be found on pages 23-24 in the IG. Student response should be based on the four definitions provided: Ball, 2018; Loversidge, 2016; Oxman et al., 2009, p. 1; and World Health Organization, 2018. In addition, the student response should address the guidance as noted in the IG on page 24: "Was the student able to differentiate evidence-based from evidence-informed? For example, was the student able to describe how clinical practice should be based on sound evidence to meet tests of safety and ethical practice, where the policy environment is complex, and evidence is used to inform the dialogue?"

3. Describe the various levels of the EBM pyramid and provide one example of the use of hierarchical evidence in policymaking. The answer will include a listing and very brief description of the seven levels of the pyramid with a statement indicating the strongest evidence is generally at the top. The seven levels, as noted on page 11 of the SW are systematic reviews (SR) at the top, followed by (in order top to bottom): critically appraised topics (evidence synthesis), critically appraised individual articles (article synopses), randomized controlled trials, cohort studies, case-controlled studies/case series/reports, and background information/expert opinion. An example of the use of hierarchical evidence in policymaking can be found within the table provided in the example of Bicycle Helmet Law on page 13 in the SW—the student should provide a unique example like any one row of the provided example.

4. Identify at least two key sources that are helpful in guiding users to evaluate evidence and provide at least one example of how at least one of sources has been used in evidence evaluation. According to the textbook, three sources useful in guiding users to evaluate evidence are 1) World Health Organization Grading of Recommendations Assessment Development and Evaluation system, 2) The Campbell Collaboration, and 3) Results for America (Loversidge and Zurmehly, 2020, p. 29). The student should identify two of the three as provided. Then the student needs to provide one example related to one of the two sources listed. The WHO Grade System has been used to evaluate clinical practice guidelines and health technology assessments (Loversidge and Zurmehly, 2020, p. 29). The Campbell Collaboration has provided evaluation on a variety of health policy issues including nutrition (Loversidge and Zurmehly, 2020, p. 30). The Results for America organization has provided a variety of evidence-based reports to guide policymaking on topics such as teen pregnancy. The Results for America organization also published a report titled "9 Ways to Make Federal Legislation Evidence-Based 2019 What Works Guide for Congress" to serve as a guide to Congress in using evidence to inform policymaking (Loversidge and Zurmehly, 2020, p. 31).

5. Compare and contrast health policy as an entity or a process by identifying key elements or keywords. (From SW page 14.) Refer to the chart on pages 29–30 in the IG.

6. Differentiate between big P health policy and little p health policy and provide an example of each (from the SW page 15). Refer to pages 31 and 32 in the IG, specifically the chart.

PAPER

Brief annotated bibliography in table format specific to a student-identified health policy problem.

LEARNING ACTIVITY

Assign the learning activity in the SW on pages 11–12. The student must include a minimum of four articles. See table on page 26 of the IG for an example.

QUIZ

1. Create a quiz focused on differentiation between policy as an entity and policy as a process. The activity on page 14 of the SW can serve as the foundation for this quiz. This would be a 10-item matching quiz. Match each statement to either entity or process. See pages 29 and 30 of the IG for answers.

2. Create a quiz focused on distinguishing among government policy, nongovernment policy, and policy at the intersection of the two. The activity on page 15 of the SW can serve as the foundation for developing this quiz. This would be a 12-item matching quiz. Match each statement to big P, little p, or intersection Pp. See pages 31 and 32 of the IG for answers.

3. Create a 22-item quiz by combining 1 and 2. See pages 29, 30, 31, 32 of the IG for answers.

THE EVOLUTION OF LEADERSHIP THEORIES

REFLECTIVE QUESTIONS

1. How are Collaborative Leadership Theory and Complexity Leadership Theory similar? Different?

    Answer: Collaborative talents and processes are both needed in a complex and changing world. The complexity leadership reflects the situation's complexity and attempts to include the conditions triggered by chaos in the complex organizational structure. The complex adaptive systems require competency and understanding of the emerging chaos and problems. Collaborative leadership refers to the collaborative process of decision-making, leading, and practicing—the leadership of the process instead of groups. Collaborative leadership aims to establish continuous collaboration.

2. What leadership style might be most effective in a situation where immediate action is required? Why?

    Answer: Authoritarian/Autocratic. Emergency situations don't allow time for extensive consultation and group decision-making. Safety first.

3. What are the four characteristics of transformational leaders?

    Answer:

    Charisma

    Inspirational motivation

    Intellectual stimulation

    Individualized consideration

4. According to Situational Leadership Theory, what factors determine the appropriate leadership style?

    Answer:

    > Task behavior
    >
    > Relational behavior
    >
    > Subordinates' maturity level

5. Explain how Behavioral Leadership Theory is different from Trait Leadership Theory.

    Answer:

    > Trait Leadership Theory: Leaders are born.
    >
    > Behavioral Leadership Theory: Behaviors can be trained (i.e., individuals can learn to lead).

NARRATIVE

As a result of the COVID-19 pandemic, the healthcare industry has seen unprecedented disruption in its priorities, operations, and outcomes, challenging leadership and management to be much nimbler. Numerous changes in hospital patient population and services available have shifted to accommodate the influx of often seriously ill COVID-19 patients. At one hospital, all ancillary operations— outpatient surgery, hospice, wellness centers, community outreach, etc.— were closed and those staff either "rifted" or reassigned.

Your unit manager is preparing to move 25% of the nursing staff to help cover the growing COVID-19 units. At a staff meeting, the manager informs the group that this will be done by lottery, and anyone selected who refuses to go will be terminated.

Your friend who works on another unit informs you that his manager plans to poll all nurses to ascertain their thoughts and willingness to take on this new assignment and, if needed, confer individually with staff before making decisions.

Another colleague reported that her manager informed staff that it would be up to them to decide who would go to the COVID-19 units and that the group decision would be final.

What management styles are these three managers exhibiting?

RESPONSE TO THE NARRATIVE

> Manager 1: Authoritarian
>
> Manager 2: Democratic
>
> Manager 3: Laissez-faire

QUIZ QUESTIONS

1. Charismatic leaders are those who have a personality that is appealing, attractive, and influential to followers.

    a) True

    b) False

    Correct Answer: a

2. Trait theorists believe that leadership behaviors can be trained.

    a) True

    b) False

    Correct Answer: b

3. The Michigan Leadership Studies in the 1950s focused on supervisory behaviors and employee productivity and satisfaction.

    a) True

    b) False

    Correct Answer: a

4. The premise of contingency theories is that leadership success is situational.

    a) True

    b) False

    Correct Answer: a

5. Situational Leadership Theory contends that a static method of leading can be effective in varied circumstances.

    a) True

    b) False

    Correct Answer: b

6. Which of the following is not a characteristic of a servant leader?

    a) Listening

    b) Empathy

    c) Prudence

    d) Charisma

    e) Commitment

    Correct Answer: d

7. The Great Man Theory from the mid-late 1800s:

    a) Emerged from biographies of great men

    b) Asserted that great men are born, not made

    c) Described leadership as an immutable property gifted to exceptional people

    d) Ignited the interest in studying the qualities of leadership

    e) Believed one's leadership ability is innate

    f) All the above

    Correct Answer: f

8. In the evolution of leadership theories, which theory came first:

    a) Path-Goal

    b) Trait Leadership Theory

    c) Behavioral Leadership Theory

    d) Transformational Leadership Theory

    e) Servant Leadership Theory

    Correct Answer: b

9. Studies that examined the relationships between supervisors' behaviors and employees' productivity and satisfaction were:

    a) Ohio State University Studies

    b) Lewin's Behavioral Study

    c) Michigan Leadership Studies

    e) Blake and Mouton Managerial Leadership Grid Studies

    Correct Answer: c

10. Fiedler's Contingency Theory from the 1960s identified which two leadership styles? (choose all that apply)

    a) Task-oriented

    b) Directive

    c) Relation-oriented

    d) Decision-making

    e) Situational

    Correct Answer: a, c

2

GLOBAL PERSPECTIVES ON THE EVOLUTION OF NURSING LEADERSHIP

REFLECTIVE QUESTIONS

1. Identify a leader who influenced your own leadership journey. What stood out? What is an example of how this person has helped shape you as a nurse leader?

   Answer: Answer should demonstrate learner has reflected on their experience, identified a person that influenced their leadership journey, what this meant to them, and how it influenced them as a leader.

2. How did the global pandemic reveal your leadership capacity? What values and beliefs guided you?

   Answer: Answer should demonstrate learner has reflected on their leadership capacity and identified their values and beliefs.

3. What leadership lessons will you take from your experiences during the COVID-19 pandemic? How will you look back five years or even 10 years from now to reflect on this stage of your leadership journey?

   Answer: Answer should demonstrate learner has identified leadership lessons and how reflection supports them in making meaning of experiences.

4. How do leaders practice inclusive principles to help everyone feel they belong?

   Answer: Leaders who practice inclusive principles lead with integrity, practice equity, are authentic, and connect with and celebrate everyone.

5.   When is a time that you felt excluded or ignored by your leader? How did you respond? What have you learned from this chapter to guide a future response?

Answer: Answer should demonstrate learner has shared feeling(s) of being ignored, how they responded, and what they learned from the readings to guide future responses.

NARRATIVE

Jennie notices that her post-operative patient has developed a urinary tract infection (UTI). She checks the chart and notes the number of days since the tubing had been changed, but no date is on the tubing. She sighs as she considers this lack of attentive nursing care. Jennie remembers that another nurse had also commented on the increase in UTIs. After confirming the standards of care for post-operative patients with an in-dwelling urinary catheter, Jennie found the other nurse and discussed her concern that the unit nurses may be slack in consistently following the evidence-based guidelines for catheter care. Should they speak up? Jennie has only been working on the unit for a year. She wonders if she has the leadership skills for bringing this to the unit council. Should she ask to lead a quality improvement project? She tries to recall leadership principles from her undergraduate program. While she feels inadequate, knowing that patients experienced unnecessary pain and suffering with a preventable UTI violates her values of quality, patient-centered care.

- What steps should Jennie take next?

- What leadership principles can help guide her actions?

- What are ways novice leaders can become more confident in their leadership?

RESPONSE TO THE NARRATIVE

Insightful responses include a discussion of disciplinary and professional knowledge, values and concepts of nursing leadership that guide decision-making. Consideration of how nurse leaders embrace lifelong learning, engage in reflective practice, and seek out additional leadership development opportunities are all key to increasing confidence.

NARRATIVE

Jennie's supervisor, Sharon, the unit director, was new, having only worked on the unit two months. Her vision was to work towards a unit with high-quality standards, establish open communication among all team members, and develop trusting and respectful relationships with staff, patients, and other disciplines. As she reviewed the unit data, she noted the increase in UTIs. She wondered when the unit standards had been last reviewed and whether nurses were adhering to the standards. Should she create a CAUTI improvement team to take a deep dive into the issue to determine next steps? How would she be able to recruit staff to participate given they were short-staffed and everyone was still on edge due to increased pressures from the COVID-19 pandemic? She thought about the various stakeholders including physicians who may have an interest and share her passion to eliminate this preventable patient harm.

- What steps should Sharon take next?

- What leadership principles can help guide her actions?

- What are ways she can establish an interprofessional team to investigate and design an improvement strategy?

- Although Jennie and Sharon are at different stages of their careers, each is facing new leadership challenges. What are similarities and differences in possible approaches for each of them?

RESPONSE TO THE NARRATIVE

Answer: Responses should include consideration of principles of leadership, health policy, teamwork, and interprofessional collaborative practices to guide decision-making.

QUIZ QUESTIONS

1. What are ways for nurses to demonstrate leadership in influencing standards, guidelines, and policies that direct practice?

    a) Become informed of latest evidence on the topic of concern

    b) Apply evidence-based practice guidelines to distill best practices

    c) Enlist co-workers to join quality improvement team

    d) Collect case examples of how changing standards makes a difference

    e) All the above

    Correct Answer: e

2. Characteristic of authentic leaders include:

    a) Ability to develop trust

    b) Ability to improve individual and team performance

    c) Value the input of others

    d) Truthfulness and openness

    e) All the above

    Correct Answer: e

3. Leadership rooted in complexity science reveals the challenge of modern healthcare delivery with three primary constructs that include:

    a) Awakening, Connector, and Upholder

    b) Awakening, Builder, and Upholder

    c) Builder, Enhancer, and Sustainer

    d) Awakening, Enhancing, and Sustaining

    Correct Answer: a

4. Three attributes of nurse leaders who embody caring competencies in order to build healthy work environments include:

    a) Communication, keeping commitments, and building and sustaining trust

    b) Communication, relationship management, and building and sustaining trust

    c) Building and sustaining trust, communication, and embracing diversity

    d) Relationship management, discovering potential, and keeping commitments

    Correct Answer: b

5. Nursing leadership attributes that contribute to development and sustainability of a healthy work environment include:

    a) Developing collaboration

    b) Professional development

    c) Emotional intelligence

    d) Organizational climate

    e) All the above

    Correct Answer: e

6. Describe how caring-based leadership is visible to others through the behaviors of the nurse leader.

    Answer: Grounded in the internal work of self-reflection, caring leaders model care and compassion for self and others, develop authentic trusting relationships, inspire collaboration, and build connections. They are lifelong learners and create environments were others want to belong.

7. Discuss how global nursing leadership is helping to shape the future of healthcare.

    Answer: Increased public recognition, scholarly publications, professional organizations supporting the development of global leaders, healthcare organizations and policy board including nurses.

8. Explore common threads of progressive models of nursing leadership.

    Answer: Common threads across servant, authentic, congruent, caring, compassion, relational, and person-centered leadership are the feeling of being valued, shared values, respect, common visions and purpose, clear roles and responsibilities, team processes, and communication skills.

9. How would you apply relational coordination in leading interprofessional teams?

    Answer: Both interprofessional leadership and relational coordination operate on principles of shared goals, mutual respect for each team member, and open communication. Both drive clear pathways, offer shared decision- making, impact patient outcomes, and improve worker satisfaction.

10.   What are differences between leadership and management?

Answer: These overlapping terms have unique roles. Leaders are intentional, turn vision to action, focus on people, motivate others to join in the mission, and serve as change agents. Managers focus on operations, systems and processes, and their position.

3

TRANSCENDING LEADERSHIP AND REDEFINING SUCCESS

REFLECTIVE QUESTIONS

1. What type of environment cultivates leadership, and which theory is applicable to this type of environment?

   Answer: The optimal environment for cultivating leadership is one that is adaptable to change. Open environments, where the adaptable elements interact broadly with both the outside world as well as within the organization, are more likely to succeed. The theory of weak ties is relevant to an adapting and changing environment because it suggests that relationships with others who have a more distant connection provide leaders with important information that leads to new ideas, innovation, and connections.

2. A leader is no longer viewed as the captain of the ship but rather as a gardener. How does a gardener represent leadership?

   Answer: Gardeners start off by selecting the right plants, and they avoid a monoculture, which means they choose a variety of plants and avoid all the same type. They recognize the elements of the environment they can control and those they cannot control. Those they can control may include the amount of compost used; those they cannot control may include the amount of rainfall, the amount of sunlight, or even the number of pests. Lastly, they create a nurturing environment for growth; therefore, just like the gardener created the best from the uncontrollable natural system, so does a leader. A leader leads their followers, those of a variety of backgrounds, in an accommodating yet changing environment, allowing individuals to grow in their profession while yielding new ideas and innovation.

3. What are the five social qualities used to determine the leader and her employees' reactions? What is the biological impact and response of these qualities on the body?

    Answer: The five social qualities used to determine the leader and his employees' reactions are status, certainty, autonomy, relatedness, and fairness. Status can either increase or decrease cortisol release, yielding a reward of longevity, health, and calmness or a threat of anxiety or stress. Certainty can enhance or inhibit neural connections and enhance or inhibit adrenaline and dopamine release, resulting in a reward of confidence and innovation, or production or a threat of diminished memory, disengagement, or a sense of being overwhelmed. Autonomy can increase or decrease adrenaline and dopamine release, yielding a reward of calmness and better decision-making or a threat of stress, disruption, and disengagement. Relatedness can cause an oxytocin release and increase endorphins, causing a reward of friendliness, collaboration, and generosity; a lack of relatedness and decreased endorphins yields a threat of being lonely, isolated, and rejected. Lastly, fairness can increase or decrease endorphins, yielding a reward of loyalty, engagement, and trust or a threat of distrust and disruption.

4. How does Kouzes and Posner's five methods of leadership development affect complex adaptive systems and neuroscience?

    Answer: Complex adaptive systems and neuroscience are reflected in the Kouzes and Posner five methods of leadership development because successful leaders and those who seek leadership positions need to understand the work environment as a complex adaptive system populated by humans with highly evolved reward and threat response systems. Understanding the implications of these reward/threat response systems and how the Kouzes and Posner model incorporates these other areas of science will lead to more effective leadership.

5. What facets must be considered for leadership development?

    Answer: Leadership development needs to include both the personal/anecdotal and the evidence-based approaches while recognizing how change occurs within a complex adaptive system and in response to the neuroscience. As a result, leaders need to be exquisitely aware of their own state of being and deeply authentic; this will require deep reflection, experiential learning, and coaching to consider how one comes across.

NARRATIVE

Jan has been a nurse for nine months; she works in a 30-bed intensive care unit. Typically, there are 17 nurses and one charge nurse on the unit during each shift, and the night shift charge nurse has been there for eight years; however, this night looks different. Tonight, there are only 14 nurses, 22 patients with the potential for eight admissions, and Jan was pulled to the charge nurse position with the possibility of having her own patient(s), depending on the number of admissions and the acuity of the patients. Jan was shifted to the charge role because she has the most experience on nights compared to the other nursing staff. The other nursing staff consists of four nurses who have six months of experience, and the others are newly off orientation. Jan is nervous about being the charge nurse for the night because she fears her experience is not enough to lead the team, and she has not had an orientation to the role. The night shift team senses her nervousness and anxiety.

RESPONSE TO THE NARRATIVE

1. Five social qualities determine the leader and the employee's reactions: status, certainty, autonomy, relatedness, and fairness. How do these qualities affect both Jan and the team?

    Answer: Status affects both Jan and the team. As a nurse with only nine months of experience, Jan feels that she is not prepared to be the charge nurse for the night shift; therefore, she feels anxious and stressed. As for the night shift team, they are a novice team, and with a leader who is anxious and stressed, they will sense her lack of confidence and begin to feel anxious.

    Certainty affects both Jan and the team. As Jan feels underprepared and anxious, she becomes overwhelmed by her role, staff, and patients. As her anxiety increases throughout the night, her team will sense that Jan feels uneasy, and they will continue to feel anxious and become overwhelmed.

    Autonomy affects both Jan and the team. Jan's stress level will increase with each admission because she will struggle to assign very sick patients to her novice staff. As Jan's stress climbs, this will disrupt her job and the flow of the unit, which could cause her to disengage from her team and responsibilities. If Jan gets to the point of being disengaged, this affects her staff because Jan's demeanor will negatively impact the staff. The staff could feel a sense of pressure, causing them to shut down and become disengaged.

    Relatedness affects both Jan and the team. Throughout the night, Jan feels overwhelmed and underprepared, but then something happens to affect the flow of the unit. For instance, if the unit gets three admissions at once or if there is a code, Jan feels like she cannot turn to anyone for assistance or direction because her staff lacks the experience needed to help; therefore, Jan begins to isolate herself from her peers, and she becomes lonely. As Jan isolates herself, the staff sense her withdrawing, and they are negatively impacted. They feel isolated and unsupported as a staff.

    Fairness affects both Jan and the team. Jan felt underprepared for this night; therefore, she may have difficulty trusting management because they put her in an uncomfortable and even unsafe situation. Just as Jan struggles with trust, so does the night shift team. The night shift team may have a hard time trusting Jan because Jan did not rely on them, and she pulled away from the team, causing a sense of mistrust between the night shift staff and Jan.

2. What elements of a complex adaptive system influences this unit and this situation?

    Answer: The elements of a complex adaptive system influencing this unit and this situation are co-evolution, inherent order, non-linearity, and unpredictability. For instance, co-evolution occurs when there is constant tension and balance within the complex adaptive system; however, in this case, the tension seemed to overpower the balance. As for inherent order, the order is maintained within the complex adaptive system. Even though the order was known (the charge nurse leading the other night shift staff) and maintained, the team leader was not prepared for her role. Non-linearity occurs when the cause-and-effect relationship is not directly linear; therefore, as Jan was settling into her role, as the other nurses were doing their jobs and as new patients were being admitted, things were constantly changing within the unit, and the effects of those things were not linear to one another. Lastly, unpredictability occurs because elements are changing, and there is no direct trajectory of the outcome. In this case, Jan was learning a new role and adjusting to her role throughout the night, the night shift nurses were adjusting and adapting to Jan's leadership, and patients were being admitted to the unit; therefore, the result was not predicted; instead, it was ever-changing.

3. Based on neuroleadership, what steps can be taken to improve the situation and the overall reactions of Jan and the team?

Answer: Neuroleadership provides individuals with the skills needed to lead effectively; therefore, when new individuals are placed into leadership roles or positions, we need to ensure they are properly trained and well equipped for the role for them to succeed. For instance, in this situation, Jan did not have proper training or the necessary tools to be in charge. She was set up to fail from the beginning. For Jan, formal training may have included a course on leadership and working with a charge nurse to learn the new role. For instance, Jan could have followed a charge nurse for several shifts to see how the charge nurse leads their team, assists with admissions, manages the charge role with a patient assignment, and maintains the department's flow. As Jan feels comfortable in this new leadership role, she could be placed in the charge role, with a backup charge nurse or nurses on shift; therefore, if Jan was not sure how to handle an issue, she could utilize the other nurses as a resource for addressing the situation. Other resources beneficial to the role of charge nurse would be a handbook or guide for the charge nurse role; the nursing supervisor's number for further assistance, especially on the night shift; and the number of the nurse manager on call to assist when things are too much for the charge nurse.

4. What steps can be taken to ensure those who are shifted into leadership roles are well equipped and well trained for success?

Answer: As individuals shift into new leadership roles, they need to be prepared appropriately and adequately trained to ensure success. Some necessary steps:

a) Before any training, have the individual take a pre-assessment survey to determine their current leadership style and skills.

b) Take a leadership course depending on the role the new individual will be getting (e.g., charge nurse course, manager course, director course).

c) Pair the individual with a preceptor. The individual preparing for the new role will be partnered with someone in the current position to ensure proper training. This period could take 8 to 16 weeks, depending on the individual and the role in which they are training.

d) As the individual becomes comfortable in the new role, assign them to the new position with the preceptor on the floor. Then, if the new hire has questions, they can seek the guidance of their preceptor. This period could be a few shifts to several shifts depending on the individual, the role, and the allotted time frame for training.

e) Upon completion of the training, have the individual take a post-assessment survey to see how much they have grown and to determine where they need continued growth.

f) As the individual is adjusting to the new role, over the next 90 days, have several check-ins to ensure they are continuing to grow in the areas specified on the post-assessment.

g) Have a three-month and six-month follow-up to ensure the individual is adjusting to their new role and see how they are enjoying their new role.

QUIZ QUESTIONS

1. What things do the new models of leadership development incorporate? (select all that apply)

    a) Knowledge from both professional experience and evidence-based

    b) Recognizing the impact of complex adaptive systems on the organization

    c) Incorporating the neuroscience of interpersonal relationships among leaders and their followers

    d) Employing Sustainable Development Goals (SDGs) in leadership development and actions

    Correct Answer: b, c

2. A good leader recognizes the extent of their influence and how change occurs in a non-linear or unpredictable system.

    a) True

    b) False

    Correct Answer: a

3. Experienced behavior is a feature of complex adaptive systems represented by constant innovation and creativity.

    a) True

    b) False

    Correct Answer: b

4. What are the key elements of complex adaptive systems (CAS) for leaders to understand?

    a) Linearity and unpredictability

    b) Nonlinearity and unpredictability

    c) Linearity and predictability

    d) Nonlinearity and predictability

    Correct Answer: b

5. Implications of leadership include which of the following? (select all that apply)

    a) Value individuality versus the interprofessional approach

    b) Emphasize the importance of a learning environment where things are tried and some work and some do not; expecting and welcoming failure leads to a learning environment

       c) Discourage self-organization

       d) Recognize different perspectives as a good thing and that a healthy level of conflict promotes progress

Correct Answer: b, d

6. What are the five reactions of the SCARF model?

       a) Status, Change, Autonomy, Relatedness, and Fairness

       b) Status, Certainty, Autonomy, Relatedness, and Fairness

       c) Status, Change, Adaptability, Relatedness, and Fairness

       d) Status, Certainty, Autonomy, Responsibility, and Fairness

Correct Answer: b

7. Five social qualities were found to determine the leader and the employees' reactions. One social quality affecting reaction is status. Status can be beneficial or threatening. A benefit of status is longevity while a threat is stress.

       a) True

       b) False

Correct Answer: a

8. Five social qualities were found to determine the leader and the employee's reactions. One social quality affecting reaction is fairness. Fairness can be beneficial or threatening. A benefit of fairness is being calm while a threat is being disengaged.

       a) True

       b) False

Correct Answer: b

9. Navigating the human psyche requires leaders to "speak" to which of the following functions in order to achieve success? (select all that apply)

       a) Thinking

       b) Feeling

       c) Learning

       d) Behaving

Correct Answer: a, b, d

10. There is evidence from psychology and organizational behavior that a leader's mental and emotional state will be reflected by their followers.

       a) True

       b) False

Correct Answer: a

4

DEVELOPING EFFECTIVE LEADERSHIP SKILLS AND CAPACITY

REFLECTIVE QUESTIONS

1. What are factors critical to the development of strengths-based leadership for nurse leaders?

    Answer: Research identified the following factors contributing to developing strengths-based leadership by nursing leaders:

    a) Valuing the whole while recognizing the inter-relationship of the parts

    b) Recognizing the uniqueness of all team roles as well as the organization's role

    c) Creating a healthy work environment that promotes development

    d) Understanding subjective reality and the need for meaning

    e) Recognizing that the person and the environment should complement the work done and capitalize on the strengths that are associated with a good fit

    f) Promoting learning and recognize that readiness and timing are essential to success

2. Please describe the sources of power in organizations.

    Answer: Based on the research identified in the chapter, the sources of power include:

    a) Coercive power—a perceived or actual fear of one person by another

    b) Reward power—the belief that someone may bestow a reward or favor

    c) Legitimate (or positional) power—power associated with an organizational position

    d) Expert power—the power derived from an individual's expertise or unique talents

    e) Referent power—the power generated from association with another

f) Information power—the belief that one has power based on what special information the person has

g) Connection power—the power derived from being connected with an individual or organization

h) Empowerment—a source of power when one in power shares authority and/or influence.

3. What are the key components of leadership's effective communication?

Answer: Based on the chapter's description, leaders need to consider the following aspects when sending messages:

a) The target audience

b) The message

c) The time and frequencies to send the message

d) Potential impacts on the target audience

e) The best communication method

4. Please describe the five modes to solve conflicts.

Answer: Researchers identified five modes for conflict management:

a) Competing: placing one's concerns ahead of others'

b) Accommodating: placing others' concerns over your own

c) Avoiding: not dealing with the conflict

d) Collaborating: working together to come to a resolution

e) Compromising: solving the conflict through partial fulfillment of one another's needs

5. What is positive leadership?

Answer: Positive leadership is an emerging leadership practice, evolving with the field of positive psychology. It refers to the performance in which leaders facilitate optimistic transformations, cultivate favorable organizational cultures, and bring out the best of human conditions. Positive leadership focuses on building human relationships and well-being and creating abundance gaps, the difference between ordinary and extraordinary performance. The strategies and practices of positive leadership can foster positivity and meaningful work and inspire followers to perform and accomplish.

NARRATIVE

One Monday morning, when Megan, the nurse manager of a surgical unit, stepped into the unit, she saw that everyone was busy. She noticed that the unit code cart was parked outside Room 1, and the code team was in the room. She was informed that a new nurse administered the wrong dose of medicine to the patient in Room 1. The patient was transferred to the ICU after the code. Once things had calmed down, Megan called the nurse to her office and asked, "What happened?" The nurse said, "I was very busy with my patients and heard other nurses talking about me. I kept thinking about what they had said about me. I was upset. I was distracted and pulled the wrong dose of medicine." Megan could tell the nurse felt terrible, and then she mumbled, "I want them to like me. I should not be distracted by them." Megan did not understand what the nurse meant and questioned the nurse, "What are you talking about?"

In the following few days, the nurse called out sick. A few weeks later, the nurse submitted her resignation letter to Megan and left the unit. A few other nurses also left the unit consecutively. Megan started to realize the necessity to evaluate the unit's work environment. She recognized a need for a change in culture in her unit.

RESPONSE TO THE NARRATIVE

What should the nurse manager, Megan, do in response to her unit's situation? Megan starts the change from the following aspects:

1. **Communication:** Instead of entirely depending on emails to communicate, she schedules with nurses and talks to them individually. She wants to know her nurses and determines their visions, goals, needs, and motivations.

2. **Conflict management:** Megan realizes that not all conflicts are destructive. If managed appropriately, conflicts can be used to motivate relationship building. She plans not to avoid conflicts but face them collaboratively to improve team building and teamwork.

3. **Strengths-based leadership:** Megan decides to apply strengths-based leadership. She invites the unit nurses to assess their strengths and use their strengths to help the unit, cultivating nurses' ownership mentality, responsibility, and engagement.

4. **Positivity building:** There is a problem with nursing staff's turnover, retention, and absenteeism. The work unit's climate is filled with negativity. Megan begins the change by changing herself. She starts to use more positive language and recognizes others often. Nurses begin to change as well. Instead of focusing on the adverse events, they begin the shift change with three positive things that happened in the previous shift. In addition, based on nurses' strengths, Megan invites two nurses—one new-graduate nurse and one mid-age nurse—to create a bulletin board to post nurses' gratitude and kind deeds.

In this narrative, Megan fosters a positive work culture in her unit based on AACN's Healthy Work Environment framework. She aims to change her unit's culture and promote nursing staff's relationship, teamwork, retention, and ultimately, patient care quality.

QUIZ QUESTIONS

1. The basis of strengths-based leadership is _____.

    a) Identifying and minimizing weaknesses

    b) Working with an executive coach

    c) Maximizing identified strengths

    d) Completing a course on strengths in leadership

    Correct Answer: c

2. Self-development based on strengths-based leadership includes all the following except _____.

    a) Ignoring blind spots, as they are a weakness

    b) Working with a peer to obtain feedback on interactions

    c) Reflection on what went well

    d) Lifelong learning

    Correct Answer: a

3. Organizational politics are not important if you work hard and do a good job.

    a) True

    b) False

    Correct Answer: b

4. Involvement in Big "P" politics involves the following except_____:

    a) Volunteering for the legislative committee of a professional organization

    b) Working on a political campaign

    c) Writing legislators regarding proposed healthcare legislation

    d) Reading the information sent out by professional organizations and voting

    Correct Answer: d

5. Development of a power base is important in organizations and may be enhanced by _____.

    a) Developing relationships with influential leaders

    b) Displaying confidence and competence in an area of importance

    c) Being conscientious in completing all tasks

    d) All the above

    e) a & b only

    Correct Answer: e

6. Power generated by association with another is _____.

    a) Expert power

    b) Referent power

    c) Coercive power

    d) Influence power

Correct Answer: b

7. All the following are examples of human capital except _____.

    a) Position capital

    b) Political capital

    c) Social capital

    d) Intellectual capital

Correct Answer: a

8. A communication model that incorporates sender, receiver, message, life experiences, culture, values, and education is called _____.

    a) Linear Model

    b) Interactional Model

    c) Teleport Model

    d) Systems Model

Correct Answer: d

9. All the following are key areas leaders should consider when drafting a message except _____.

    a) Message (what needs to be conveyed)

    b) Method of message (e.g., in-person, written, etc.)

    c) Time of message

    d) Teleport model

Correct Answer: d

10. In 2001, the American Association of Critical-Care Nurses began promoting a framework called _____ to combat horizontal violence in the workplace.

    a) Healthy Work Environment

    b) Transactional Model

    c) COPE Model

    d) SWOT Analysis

Correct Answer: a

11. An important element of a team's cohesion is _____.

 a) Diversity

 b) Trust

 c) Location

 d) Number of members

Correct Answer: b

12. One major change in team dynamics due to the COVID-19 pandemic is _____.

 a) Dress code

 b) Moving to a virtual format

 c) Time of meetings

 d) Number of members

Correct Answer: b

13. Nursing leaders mentoring virtual teams must do all the following except:

 a) Make sure policies and procedures support the team

 b) Work with Information Technology to secure the most advanced technology possible

 c) Check in with team members regularly for any needs

 d) Use emojis and encoding emotions or sound effects in message language extensively

Correct Answer: d

14. Recognizing the importance "influence" has on leadership/member interactions, which document has "influence" embedded into a competency?

 a) American Association of Critical-Care Nurses Healthy Work Environment

 b) American Organization of Nursing Leadership Nurse Executive Competencies

 c) Institute of Medicine's To Err Is Human

 d) United States government's Healthy People 2030

Correct Answer: b

15. Leadership models can help leaders focus and practice on skills to be more effective. Which of the following is an example of a leadership model a new nurse leader can utilize in practice?

 a) The Human-Centered Leadership Model

 b) Krebs Cycle Model

 c) ARC Framework (Competency, Regulation, Attachment)

 d) The IOWA Model

Correct Answer: a

5

NURTURING HEALTHY AND HEALING WORK ENVIRONMENTS

REFLECTIVE QUESTIONS

1. Reflect on theoretical nursing knowledge and your values and strengths as a nurse. How are they visible and invisible in your role as a nurse leader?

    Answer: Students should demonstrate they reflected on their knowledge, values, and strengths by identifying each and discussing how they are visible or not in their leadership practices.

2. What intentional healing practices do you use that demonstrate care for yourself? For others?

    Answer: Students identify intentional practices that are meaningful to them and others.

3. How do you currently use reflective practice in your personal and professional life? What more can you do? Why does it matter?

    Answer: Students identify how they use reflective practice or not in their personal and professional life, what more they can do, and why it matters to them.

4. Describe the landscape of your current healthcare environment. What is the most important step you can take, as a leader, to integrate healing practices into the environment?

    Answer: Students describe the landscape of their healthcare environment and healing practices they can incorporate in it.

5. How does your well-being influence you and your role as a nurse leader who develops and applies nursing knowledge?

Answer: Students discuss how their well-being influences their ability to show up for others in a way that incorporates and applies nursing knowledge.

NARRATIVE

You are a nurse manager on an inpatient medical-surgical unit and have been in your position for two years. While the clinical environment is beginning to settle into a new normal after COVID-19, you have lost a number of staff and experienced changes at the bedside at a more rapid pace than before. At the same time, the organization is requesting you start a number of new quality and safety initiatives, and you are faced with competing priorities. In addition to a stressful environment, you have very little time to yourself or to check in with staff due to being in meetings all day long. You get home to receive a call that the unit is short-staffed with three nurses for 24 patients. You have a six-month-old baby at home and want to spend time with your family but feel guilty leaving your nurses short-staffed. These types of situations are occurring more and more frequently at work. What intentional practices will help you navigate care for yourself and others, and influence the organization to create a more healing environment?

RESPONSE TO THE NARRATIVE

The nurse leader will engage in various self-care practices such as mindfulness, reflective practice, being authentic and identifying values, direct and transparent communication, modeling the way for others, and creating iterative practices within a team environment to support individual and collective growth. Priorities are re-established, and nurse-led initiatives are developed to integrate the organizational values within a healing environment.

QUIZ QUESTIONS

1. Attending to the healing process is ultimately what will result in a healthy and healing work environment.

    a) True

    b) False

    Correct Answer: a

2. Which of the following are elements of a healthy work environment?

    a) Fosters self-care and well-being

    b) Safe

    c) Empowering

    d) Evidence-based practice education

    e) All the above

    Correct Answer: e

    Rationale: All the above elements are described in the literature as elements for creating a healthy work environment and are included within the Essentials for Magnetism studies.

3. It is the responsibility of the nurse to develop a healthy work environment.

    a) True

    b) False

    Correct Answer: b

    Rationale: It is both an individual nurse's responsibility and the responsibility of the organizations and leaders that make up the system to create healthy work environments.

4. Which theorist highlights the importance of being present when interacting with others, acknowledging others' viewpoints, and unfolding meaning with presence to enhance the quality of work-life both for themselves and for others?

    a) Watson

    b) Parse

    c) Palmer

    d) Watkins

    Correct Answer: b

    Rationale: Parse's theory of Human Becoming highlights the importance of the relationships within nursing and describes mindfulness as a tool for enhancing the quality of life.

5. How might one utilize and implement nursing theory and research to create healthy work environments?

    a) Theory and research provide a framework that guides inquiry.

    b) Theories should be implemented to enhance mindfulness.

    c) Testing theories and research in an organization to prove a healthy work environment.

    d) None of the above.

    Correct Answer: a

    Rationale: Theory and research act as a framework to guide further inquiry and curiosity into philosophical micro practices, which influence a healthy work environment.

6. Self-care is an iterative process.

    a) True

    b) False

    Correct Answer: a

    Rationale: Self-care is an ongoing process that requires self-reflection and evolvement to sustain.

7. Which of the following are characterized as intentional individual self-care practices?

    a) Being authentic and true to oneself

    b) Mindfulness

    c) Gratitude

    d) Self-awareness

    e) Reflective practice

    f) All the above

Correct Answer: f

Rationale: Being authentic and utilizing mindfulness, gratitude, self-awareness, and reflective practice are all intentional individual self-care practices.

8. What is the definition of mindfulness?

    a) Focusing on the future

    b) Sitting in silence

    c) Being present in the current moment without judgment

    d) Praying

Correct Answer: c

9. How does one reach a state of being rather than doing in the profession of nursing?

    a) Practicing mindfulness

    b) Any intentional practice that connects mind, body, and spirit while staying in the present

    c) Authentically connecting with others and the environment

    d) All the above

Correct Answer: d

10. What characteristics assist in authentic leadership and promote a healthy work environment? (choose all that apply)

    a) Knowing oneself, bringing values to work, and creating an empowering environment for others to share their perspectives

    b) Representing the values of the organization, even at the risk of misalignment with your values

    c) Being an effective communicator

    d) Acting as an advocate for resources for staff

Correct Answer: a, c, d

Rationale: It's important for authentic leaders to stand by their values, model self-care for others, and empower through removing obstacles.

6

LEADERSHIP ROLES IN PROMOTING A RESILIENT WORKFORCE

REFLECTIVE QUESTIONS

1. Describe the effects that compassion fatigue can have on caregivers, patients, and organizations.

   Answer: Caregivers experience fatigue, burnout, anxiety, hopelessness, and depression and can be disconnected from their purpose and meaningfulness of their role in helping others. Organizations deal with poor patient satisfaction, patient harm, dissatisfied care providers, and high turnover rates. Patients suffer the most because when compassion fatigue and burnout are prevalent, it is almost impossible for them to get the care they need. They can experience decreased healing, uncaring providers, a feeling of dehumanization, and exposure to toxic environments void of healing potential.

2. Discuss why leadership is important to resiliency when self-care is a personal practice/decision.

   Answer: Leaders create the cultures and climates of the departments they manage. While stress is inherent in caring for others, leaders contribute to the health of their teams by recognizing emotional labor as part of the job and paying attention to what their team members need to flourish. They can do this by modeling self-care, getting to know their team well enough to notice when they are getting burned out, and knowing what they need to recover.

3. List three attributes of a leader who is focused on care provider resiliency.

    Answer: A leader who is focused on resiliency should care about the care provider individually and take time to understand what motivates them, what they are passionate about, and what they need to manage stress. Empower their teams to have what they need to do their jobs. Treat everyone with respect and dignity. Recognize care providers. Lead by inspiring others to do their best without using fear or pressure. Model resiliency practices and reward team members for taking care of themselves.

4. Describe the difference in healthcare providers' experience when working on a unit that prioritizes support, resiliency, and recovery vs. a unit that does not.

    Answer: Working on the first unit does not mean that there will never be stress. It does mean that even if the shift is hard, you know you will have the resources needed and will feel supported enough to believe you will be OK regardless of what happens, compared to the other experience where your well-being may be at risk because you won't get what you need physically, emotionally, or psychologically.

5. What are some offerings that an organization can prioritize to help build a resiliency culture in healthcare?

    Answer: Recovery through art, team retreats, small support group time like in compassionate communities, theory-guided practice like Caring Science education and groups, peer-to-peer support programs, incorporating positive psychology practices into work, and building in recognition and rewards for individual participation in recovery practices both at work and outside of work hours.

NARRATIVE

Behavioral Health Specialists are responsible for direct patient care and safety, including supervision and management of children and adolescents who may be experiencing a psychiatric crisis. Behavioral Health Specialists work in diverse environments, including inpatient psychiatric units, partial hospitalization or day treatment programs, and medical floors. One Behavioral Health Specialist named Neena, working in the psychiatric department of a large children's hospital, participated in a 12-week workshop designed to create community and develop resilience using artmaking. This workshop was facilitated by an art therapist, using a sequential curriculum within a peer-reviewed research protocol. Each week, Neena attended the group, looking forward to the chance to focus on herself, her creativity, and new relationships with other providers with similar self-care goals. Neena practiced different therapeutic skills and art-making techniques, building her confidence as well as her ability to be vulnerable. On the seventh week, she was asked to visually represent an especially challenging day at work, one that she may not be able to forget. Neena created an image of the day she was physically assaulted by a patient in distress. The image included red prison bars, representing her feeling of being trapped in the situation, and a red pool of blood at the bottom, which was her own. The image itself brought Neena to tears as she shared it with the group, recounting the story that she had not shared with anyone since it happened 12 weeks prior.

The group witnessed her courage and vulnerability in this process, offering her words of support and understanding. Neena left that day exhausted but relieved to have let this trauma pour out of her onto paper. She came back the following week feeling refreshed and rejuvenated, with new purpose and perspective on her professional worth.

In the last few weeks of the group, participants were asked to share artwork and writing for a collaborative artwork, with the goal of sharing their voices beyond the intimate setting of the group. Neena wrote the following to accompany another artwork she had created, depicting another intense day:

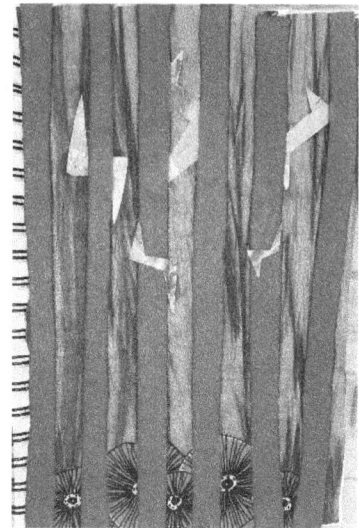

Original art by Neena, Behavioral Health Specialist

> Behind the mask, tears are streaming down my face and my adrenaline is pumping harder than it has in my entire life. I can hear my own heartbeat, and the pounding in my ears is terrifying. One of my coworkers starts counting down from 3, and I know that once we get to 1, we're releasing our grip on the door handle and entering our patient's room to put them into a supine hold. This step, while traumatic for both the patient and for staff, is necessary at this moment to maintain the safety of our patient and everyone else on our unit. Knowing that doesn't make it any easier. Once we get to 1, I have to face the reality that I may witness one or more of my coworkers getting hurt. I have to accept that I may no longer have control and could get hurt myself. I have to be the most aware and present I have ever been to ensure our patient remains safe. 3, 2, 1. I take a deep breath, and I step forward.
>
> Behind the mask, I am a Behavioral Health Specialist working on a psychiatric unit during a global pandemic. Sometimes my job is rewarding beyond what I could ever imagine. Feeling the impact we have on our patients and witnessing the changes they can make is amazing. At the same time, I have left work countless times crying, dehydrated, bruised, bleeding, or covered in bodi-

Original art by Neena, Behavioral Health Specialist

ly fluids. I've continually surprised myself with my ability to step up to the plate, but being the holder of someone else's pain and trauma is never easy and always weighs on you. Something I've taken away from our art group is that this is a shared sentiment among healthcare workers, yet we never back down. We continue to show up, day in and day out, for our patients and for our coworkers. We find ways to build resilience and we lean on each other. We step up to the plate in hard or scary situations, and that makes us brave. Throughout this group experience and my reflections on the past year of working in healthcare during a pandemic, I've been reminded that despite everything, hope and courage still persist.

After reading through the experience of the healthcare provider in the narrative, what can you appreciate about a resiliency approach that includes different creative modalities to help staff process their trauma and reconnect to their individual purpose?

RESPONSE TO THE NARRATIVE

The answer would be just a personal reflection of the need for this type of offering, so the answers will be varied.

QUIZ QUESTIONS

1. What leadership styles are complementary with promoting resiliency in healthcare providers?

    a) Transformational

    b) Servant

    c) Authentic

    d) All the above

    Correct Answer: d

2. Emotional labor measures not only the quantity of care provided but also considers the quality of the experiences of care.

    a) True

    b) False

    Correct Answer: a

3. What are important factors for leaders to pay attention to regarding how their team members recover from stress? (choose all that apply)

    a) Are they on call regardless of the time of day?

    b) As a leader I should not get involved in such personal practices.

    c) Do they answer emails even when they are on vacation?

    d) None of the above.

    Correct Answer: a, c

4. Compassion fatigue not only considers the inability to care for patients but also the distress it has on the care provider themselves.

    a) True

    b) False

    Correct Answer: a

5. Arrange the following answers in the correct order for the team-based approach to build resiliency within a department.

    a) Create a road map for action

    b) Identify core values of each team member

    c) List action items to align with each value

    d) Prioritize values among the entire team

Correct Answer: b-d-c-a

6. If I don't see myself as an artist, then using art to process stress won't work.

    a) True

    b) False

Correct Answer: b

7. What do Caring Science workshops give the participants?

    a) A time to reconnect to purpose

    b) A way to practice loving-kindness for self and others

    c) A pause to honor the unique role caregivers have in healthcare

    d) A time to be surrounded and supported by peers who understand your experiences

    e) All the above

Correct Answer: e

8. Team members will see their leader as weak if they show their own vulnerabilities and talk about what they need to build resiliency.

    a) True

    b) False

Correct Answer: b

9. One of the most important starting points for organizations to begin building a resilient workforce is to:

    a) Hire people who do not seem to be affected by stress

    b) Remind care providers that they should care for themselves outside of work

    c) Recognize emotional labor as part of choosing to become a care provider and prioritize recovery as part of the work

    d) Set up a yoga program after work hours

Correct Answer: c

10. Practicing self-care and fostering resilience are the least important priorities to consider as a healthcare provider.

      a) True

      b) False

Correct Answer: b

7

LEADERSHIP ROLES IN MITIGATING ORGANIZATIONAL TRAUMA

REFLECTIVE QUESTIONS

1. Consider an experience that made you feel traumatized at your workplace. What was the situation? What happened to you? How would you describe (a) the event, (b) the experience, (c) the effects of the workplace trauma?

    Answer: Each response will be different given individual context. Framing the question to "What happened to you?" versus "What is wrong with you?" is important to note.

2. Could you describe the strategies that leaders can use to help you heal from that trauma?

    Answer: Language creates our experience of reality, and how we choose to name things influences how we experience them and how we value them. The language of business and commerce has resulted in many traumatized organizations. The language of caring, helping, healing, and a relational language of being is needed for healing to take place (Quinn, 2002). Leaders must bring about regrowth of group well-being, which will translate into their willingness to engage with the organization (Powley & Cameron, 2006).

3. How do you as a nurse leader impact the organization and help it heal and remain a healing organization?

    Answer: Organizational healing requires attention to employees' well-being, as employees also transformed are healed. Employees' well-being can be measured by factors such as mental and physical health, psychological functioning, and demonstrated behaviors (Gallego-Toledo, 2015). At the unit level, a trauma-informed supervisor's use of secondary traumatic stress (STS) core competencies (NCTSN, 2018) offers practical advice to support healing.

4. What are your suggestions for organizational leadership teams to promote a caring-healing environment?

   Answer: Caring Science is a lens by which to reframe and revitalize an organization. Use of caring consciousness and action serves as a foundation for transforming and healing an organization that has been traumatized (Messina, 2019). Becoming whole requires a leader who embeds patterns of compassion, caring, mutual support, courage, and faith. Employees need supportive actions to heal the organization's social fabric, sense of continuity, expectations, culture, and identity. The leader will need to utilize language that signals an end of former processes and practices.

5. Describe ways to enhance organizational post-traumatic growth.

   Answer: In a parallel manner to individuals who achieve transcendence and post-traumatic growth, a new organization emerges with collective awareness and insights. Such an organization may be achieved through an approach called Appreciative Inquiry (AI) and the four cornerstone ideas behind AI: Discovery, Dream, Design, and Destiny (Cooperrider & Whitney, 1999; Fry et al., 2002; Grieten et al., 2018). AI is a strengths-based method of organizational change and has been used as a framework in healthcare organizations (Hung et al., 2018). In the context of this discussion, it is a conduit for organizational growth due to what has been gained by operationalizing trauma-informed organizational strategies. Assuming that trauma-informed practices are infused within the organization, and especially within individual staff members, it's time for leaders to move the organization to a new level of functioning where psychological safety is a given, voices are heard, and trust, forgiveness, and compassion are cultural norms. In essence, nurse leaders need to move the nursing staff toward new possibilities of existing in the present and envisioning a new future.

NARRATIVE

Jameson Hospital is a 530-bed acute care hospital. The critical care unit has 12 beds and is typically 90% occupied. Typically, there are six nurses on each shift. On a Thursday night, the unit had 12 patients and one of the night shift nurses had called in, leaving five nurses on duty to work 7 pm to 7 am. During the shift, Nancy grabbed some medication and cross checked it with Sarah. Nancy went into room 12 and administered the medication; within minutes the patient went into V-fib. A code was called and during the middle of resuscitation, Nancy realized she had pulled the wrong dosage of the medication resulting in the patient arresting. Nancy immediately told the physician running the code hoping that the information would help save the patient. The patient died. The family was informed of the death. However, no one informed the family of the cause of the death. The organization reported both Nancy and Sarah to the Board of Nursing, resulting in Nancy losing her license and Sarah being placed on probation. The nursing staff slowly became aware of what had happened as both nurses were friends with other nurses in the unit and everyone was heartsick over the loss of two critical care nurses, and the short staffing that everyone felt played into the outcome. The hospital administration held a staff meeting telling everyone to not discuss the case. Each week that passed, the nursing staff sunk deeper into depression. The nurse who had called out sick that night ended up resigning after four weeks, unable to take the side glances;

it seemed everyone was wondering if she had worked her shift, would this have happened? Even those nurses who worked on the night shift eventually resigned over the course of four months.

1. Describe how organizational trauma evolved in this case.

2. Discuss the cumulative impacts of organizational trauma in this scenario.

3. Describe ways of using caring consciousness and actions to promote organizational caring-healing when trauma occurs.

4. Explain how the Sanctuary Model could be utilized as a viable approach in this case.

RESPONSE TO THE NARRATIVE

1. Organizational trauma occurred when short staffing resulted in a medication error ending in a death.

2. The cumulative impact of organizational trauma included an environment that did not allow for healing. When nurses were not allowed to discuss what had occurred or how their colleague had been treated, the turnover rate increased. Eventually, the environment of shame and blame led to all the night-shift nurses quitting.

3. Using caring consciousness and actions could have been utilized to bring about healing in the organization. Steps that should have been taken include:

    a) **Embrace** a model of kindness and compassion in interactions with individuals within and outside the organization.

    b) **Inspire** faith by leaders offering optimism, confidence, and energy to help employees reconnect with the mission.

    c) **Trust** should have been cultivated by having leaders fully present. Listening and reflecting before action would have built trust through a stance of compassion. Being fully present in the moment with unconditional compassion and acceptance of others' potentially painful experiences from the loss of their colleagues would have **nurtured** the healing. A non-judgmental attitude by the leader would facilitate respectful communication. A leader should engage the staff with proactive problem solving, reframing a situation to see the potential or positive side.

    d) **Forgive** the past to allow individuals the opportunity to share their stories, and reflect on their feelings and experiences.

    e) **Deepen** ways of knowing/being/doing/becoming and commit to creatively problem solve.

    f) **Balance** is about using creativity to uncover the imagination of employees as you move toward a rebirth of the traumatized organization, which will bring about a readiness to learn. Leadership and nursing staff should **co-create** a healing environment by engaging employees with dignity and respect.

g) **Ministering** to the staff by leadership requires communication skills that provide feedback for growth and for reassurance. The leader helps employees navigate difficult times and supports decision-making processes in their organization's values.

h) **Openness** to different (infinite) possibilities is a characteristic of a leader suitable for a traumatized organization. Being open allows you to challenge ideas about how things should work. Leaders should not judge other people, as they could be closing off amazing possibilities.

4.   The Sanctuary Model could be utilized as a viable approach in this case. This approach situates both the individual, who has experienced traumatic events as well as the system, as characterized by mutual interactions (Esaki et al., 2013). The Sanctuary Model uses the acronym "SELF" to structure a common language within organizations: Safety, Emotions, Loss and Future. Identifying which of these concepts is present in a problem faced by the organization can forward solutions to addressing the difficulty.

The nurse leaders should ask the nurses how safe they feel. Debriefing after adverse events, conducting root cause analysis of the event, and acknowledging the potential trauma experienced are ways of increasing safety. Emotions need to be expressed by the nurses involved. Loss is also a part of SELF and requires everyone to share the loss they feel. The future is addressing the problem of loss, lack of safety, and the emotions which occurred because of the trauma. Together, nurse leaders and nursing staff need to envision a positive future where individuals and the organization share common trauma-informed values and address current and future problems.

QUIZ QUESTIONS

1.   Unrecognized wounding is a pattern of trauma in organizations. Which of the following is an example of unrecognized wounding?

a) An African American nurse is met with workplace violence by a patient's family members as they mutter racial slurs under their breath; her reporting of the event is minimized.

b) A school of nursing and a community hospital are at odds over an adverse event attributed to a student nurse.

c) Rumors about working conditions and constant nurse turnover cause a hospital to become even more short-staffed.

d) Gossiping, incivility, and interpersonal conflicts become the norm for organizational communication.

Correct Answer: a

Rationale: b is an example of unproductive relationships, c is an example of narrowing worldview, and d is an example of stress and anxiety contagion.

2. What would be an appropriate comment made by a trauma-informed supervisor?

    a) "In looking at your performance, I need to ask, what is wrong with you?"

    b) "Let me tell you about how badly stressed out I was! I almost couldn't function. I ended up getting fired."

    c) "I want to encourage you to reset that critical voice inside you and compare it to your actual performance."

    d) "We really need to improve on certain things. You just seem 'out of it' half the time. Care to tell me about it?"

Correct Answer: c

Rationale: The other responses are counter to providing a safe psychological space and to the ANA Code of Ethics.

3. In praxis of embracing the organization for healing, forgiveness is described. Which of the following statements best captures forgiveness within the organization?

    a) Transparency in organizational communications will allow employees to understand how decisions are made.

    b) The authentic leader speaks to optimism and energy, reminding employees of the mission of the organization.

    c) The nurse manager demonstrates presence, empathy, and benevolence toward nurses who have experienced trauma.

    d) Employees are encouraged to release the past and move forward, thereby avoiding the toxicity that can arise from holding onto old grudges and mistakes.

Correct Answer: d

Rationale: a describes the concept of trust, b describes the concept of inspiration, c describes embracing compassion and kindness.

4. Which of the following does *not* exemplify "resisting re-traumatization" in organizations?

    a) Organizational leaders revise procedures for patient assessment to include assessment of past traumatic events using trauma-informed language.

    b) Organizational leaders plan a retreat for upper managers to ensure optimal coding is in place for third party payor reimbursement.

    c) A system-wide orientation is implemented to cover basic principles of trauma-informed practices.

    d) Policies and procedures for debriefing after a workplace violence event are reviewed to ensure trauma-informed practices.

Correct Answer: b

Rationale: This intervention does not transform the organization to ensure staff and patients avoid re-traumatization.

5. Appreciative Inquiry (AI) is a way of bridging how organizations heal from trauma and envision a new, strengths-based approach. When comparing an organizational trauma-informed approach with AI, which of the following is true?

    a) Appreciative Inquiry is a strengths-based approach, while a trauma-informed approach concentrates on individual deficits.

    b) Appreciative Inquiry is a strengths-based approach, while a trauma-informed approach is one of knowledge- and skills-based strategies to process and heal from individual and collective trauma.

    c) Appreciative Inquiry and trauma-informed approaches are both deficit-based approaches.

    d) Appreciative Inquiry addresses the individual, while a trauma-informed approach is about maximizing organizational resources.

Correct Answer: b

Rationale: The other responses are false.

8

HEALTHCARE LEADERSHIP IN PLANETARY AND ENVIRONMENTAL HEALTH

REFLECTIVE QUESTIONS

1. Why might it be helpful to seek out nature when considering an important work challenge, life question, or career choice?

   Answer: Any of the 14 "gifts" (or equivalents) that are noted in the table in this chapter would be correct.

2. As nurse leaders, why is it important to consider how we, as a society, address the social determinants of health?

   Answer: Because these are the things that are either substantially helping us to be well or substantially causing us to be ill. And because they are not usually in the healthcare system's wheelhouse.

3. How did we become a society so fraught with loneliness and anxiety and how is that contributing to health risks? What can we do about this?

   Answer: Work to build community-level social capital, work collaboratively with a broad range of community stakeholders, address nature-deficit disorder in children, and any other approach that is going to help build individual and population-based resilience.

4. How might national nursing organizations begin to advocate for positive changes regarding the social determinants of health and why does that really require collective action?

   Answer: Race, poverty, education, housing, and other social determinants are going to require political and economic solutions which, in turn, will require nurses to collaborate broadly within nursing and with a range of other intersectional advocates.

5. What does the more beautiful world our hearts know is possible look like? Think expansively. Paint it as clearly as possible.

   Answer: This is a wonderful exercise for group discussion. Follow this question after they have had some time to discuss, with the next question: How do we get there?

GROUP ACTIVITY PHASE ONE

Cover large tables with craft paper (available in most teacher-supply or toy and craft stores), give each student a marker, and have the students stand around the table. Ten students per rectangular table works well.

Ask the students to take turns identifying the "systems" that make up our communities and have them describe what works and doesn't work regarding these systems and what are sometimes the unintended consequences of the systems.

Start them with the transportation system and ask them to draw the elements (e.g., roads/highways, public transportation, sidewalks, biking paths, airports, ferries, etc.).

1. What are the positive and negative effects of this system?
2. What are the health promoting aspects of this system and what are not?

RESPONSE TO FIRST PHASE OF THE ACTIVITY

The way this works is at any given table students talk about things and then one person will draw something. In the instance of transportation, one student would draw a road or two, another a bike lane/path, another an airport, and so on so that everyone begins to feel like they "co-own" the community that may include a town/city/suburbs/outskirts/agricultural lands/parkland. Lots of students will say they can't draw, but there will always be an artist among them. Let them know that stick figures, circles, and squares are all they need and encourage everyone to draw something. Generally, the process escalates so that everyone begins to contribute, and they also enjoy making fun of each other's drawings.

GROUP ACTIVITY PHASE TWO

After working with the transportation system and discussing it, see if they can think of another system to draw. For example, the health delivery system might include the school nurse, local clinics, individual doctors/NP offices, mental health facilities/practitioners, ambulances, recovery facilities, public health department, and so on. (And, of course, a hospital. But they may include a VA hospital, a county hospital, etc.)

Other systems: Parks/recreation, commerce, industry/manufacturing, public safety/judicial/jails, sanitation, communications/media, housing, education (K-12/higher), systems for special needs (elderly, cognitively impaired), food/agriculture (lots here), government, and non-governmental organizations.

The "housing" one is interesting because you can ask: "Where is everyone sleeping today/tonight?" and see how they process that question. Where are the "beds"—homes/apartments, group homes, jails, nursing homes, hotels, on the streets?

RESPONSE TO THE SECOND PHASE OF THE ACTIVITY

This is a great exercise for students to visually consider the many systems that support our modern societies and where they are sometimes failing us. It's also a good way for emerging nurse leaders to think more expansively about how we create or hinder health in the community.

QUIZ QUESTIONS

1. As outlined by Brian Mertins, who is involved in nature mentoring, which of the following can be learned in nature:

    a) Presence and Awareness

    b) Gratitude and Appreciation

    c) Relationships and Emotional Intelligence

    d) All the above

    Correct Answer: d

2. According to the World Health Organization, what percentage of global diseases are attributed to the social determinants of health?

    a) 10–25%

    b) 30–55%

    c) 60–80%

    d) 90%

    Correct Answer: b

3. The healthcare system is currently configured to address the social determinants of health.

    a) True

    b) False

    Correct Answer: b

4. What "ailment" did US Surgeon General Vivek Murthy observe to be contributing to increased mortality as much as smoking or obesity?

    a) Cancer

    b) Food insecurity

    c) Loneliness

    d) Autoimmune diseases

    Correct Answer: c

5. According to a Cigna study, more teens are feeling more socially isolated than ever before.

    a) True

    b) False

    Correct Answer: a

6. Why are the ailments noted in this chapter important for nursing leaders to know and acknowledge?

    Answer: Because these "ailments" are what are making us sick in significant ways, and the healthcare system is not currently addressing them.

7. Planetary health is a new conceptual framework that recognizes that humans should have dominion over the natural world.

    a) True

    b) False

    Correct Answer: b

8. In addition to the healthcare system, what other systems should nursing leaders understand when addressing the complex causes of disease?

    a) Economic

    b) Political

    c) Ecological

    d) All the above

    Correct Answer: d

9. Reframing our message from what we are against to what we are for will allow us to develop more hopeful messages.

    a) True

    b) False

    Correct Answer: a

10.   The use of the Mother Tree in this chapter is helpful in considering some of the basic but pro-found shifts that may be necessary to achieve human and planetary health. What are some of the shifts that you think are the most important right now?

Answer: The answer to this is somewhat subjective but might include addressing the social determinants of health, addressing environmental destruction, building stronger community social supports, or any other overarching shift that will move us to health.

QUANTUM CARING LEADERSHIP: A NEW ONTOLOGY INTO PRACTICE

REFLECTIVE QUESTIONS

1. In light of your experience and the learning from this chapter, how do you integrate the Caritas Processes into practice including care for self, others, and organization/community?

   Answer: Students provide an explanation of how they can integrate Caritas Processes into their practices for self, others, and their organization/community.

2. How is unitary consciousness visible in your role as a nurse leader? What more can you do?

   Answer: Students state how unitary consciousness is visible or invisible in their role as a nurse leader and describe what more they can do.

3. What does Quantum Caring Leadership mean to you?

   Answer: Students describe what Quantum Caring Leadership means to them.

4. How can the principles of Quantum Caring Leadership be utilized to sustain humanity?

   Answer: Students connect principles of Quantum Caring Leadership to ways to sustain humanity.

5. Why does embracing a unitary quantum caring worldview matter?

   Answer: Students explain why a unitary quantum worldview matters.

NARRATIVE

An invitation to present to the regional quality council of a large healthcare system was extended to a Chief Nurse Executive (CNE), the direct result of notable and sustained improvements in quality outcomes, operational performance, and service metrics over a two-year period.

In sharing the team's story, the CNE identified that despite dutifully implementing the same system-wide initiatives and best practices supported by detailed playbooks, checklists, and service scripts, their hospital's scorecard remained among the lowest in the region. Following extended leadership gaps and turnover, the new and current nurse executive assessed the landscape, identified a unique and disruptive opportunity, and proposed a different approach to address performance gaps that involved the integration of established Caring Science Theory and emerging Quantum Leadership principles. The leadership and clinical teams were engaged and subsequently espoused their support during open leader forums, enthusiastically embracing the vision to actively transform their culture through Quantum Caring Leadership (QCL) principles, evidence, and informed moral action.

The leadership message and commitment were that this hospital or community of leaders and care teams would begin a journey to consciously lead and act through human connections and authentic caring relationships. Conventional leadership approaches had previously focused on controlling processes, competency, metrics, and compliance. They were fostering trust, and shifting the culture required education, mentoring, coaching, and role-modeling that was both ubiquitous and aligned with QCL. Teams had to discover new ways of being and becoming together, unlearning divisive or separatist thinking and develop evolved practices that were more congruent with Quantum Caring Leadership. The focus was on supporting the ongoing development of confident, caring clinicians and leaders committed to establishing an authentic, caring, compassionate, and healing culture. Learning forums were conducted regularly to model appreciative dialogue and discover the shared meaning behind new or emerging initiatives. Change was no longer something to fear or resist but increasingly perceived as an opportunity to learn, grow, adapt, and improve care together. Clinicians were engaged every step of the way and soon adopted a credo, "Nothing about us, without us!" to represent their commitment to full engagement. In addition to authentic dialogue and intentional inclusion, decisions were no longer made in an office but encouraged and supported to be made as close to the point of care as possible. Experiential learning events on QCL, Caring Science integration, and the 10 Caritas Processes helped guide leader and care team commitments to self-care, resilience, connectedness, caring moments, and healing environments. Growing evidence of intentionality, presence, connectedness, and authentic caring connections was best reflected in narratives. Inviting and celebrating caring moments prior to meetings and in shift huddles/cuddles helped infuse a steady sense of joy and meaning in the collective work.

In closure, the CNE reinforced that hospital leaders have continually evolved and come to value their role as navigators, translators, and champions of a harmonizing QCL message that unites teams under a common vision in order to achieve uncommon results. Their commitment to relationships and connectedness helped engender trust, and through consistent QCL practices they have nurtured ongoing growth, quality, success, and the ability for patients, individuals, teams, and the organization to flourish together. Empowered through QCL practices, care teams are increasingly aware, fully engaged, and owning their practice, which has been observed to be a liberating, organic, transformative, renewable, and an indispensable source of continued success and sustained performance as a caring community.

ACTIVITY

Directions: In pairs or small groups, create a list of Quantum Caring Leadership (QCL) characteristics identified in the case study. Referring to the list of QCL characteristics, invite participants to share a leadership experience where QCL characteristics were either clearly evident or notably absent. Discuss the potential impact of sustained congruence between theory and leadership practices (QCL) on patient care, the nursing workforce, and organizational performance.

BEING, BECOMING, AND DOING AS A QCL

BEING: The quantum caring leader exists at the highly complex and continually evolving intersections of the organization. It is here that the self-aware and conscious leader must assess, sort, translate, interpret, predict, and ultimately make decisions.

BECOMING: Engagement is a dynamic, relationship-centric journey to intentionally harmonize quantum caring leader and team alignment through a shared commitment to a common mission, vision, and congruent set of values.

DOING: Living out QCL requires authentic presence, role modeling, coaching, and ongoing evaluation to nurture a continuously evolving and thriving quantum caring community.

RESPONSE TO THE NARRATIVE

Response: How leaders view the world determines their leadership style, interactions, and the work environment they directly or indirectly propagate. QCL theory, philosophy, and values are exhibited through key characteristics that value relationships, interconnectedness, and win/win dynamics. In the narrative, the QCL leader is new but quickly assesses and identifies the opportunity to bring care teams together through existing Unitary Caring Science Theory and congruent Quantum Leadership teachings and approaches. QCL principles and characteristics in the narrative reflect leadership's commitment to Caring Science integration, connectedness, caring relationships, consciousness, compassion, trust, shared meaning, authenticity, engagement, inclusion, empowerment, ongoing development, self-care, team resilience, joy, and healing environments. QCL has the potential to directly impact patient care through conscious, intentional, and fully engaged teams practicing within a Caring Science framework. The integration of Caring Science and Quantum Leadership (QCL) supports authentic caring relationships among leaders, nurses, and care teams, valuing Caritas Processes, caring moments and informed moral practices between patients, families, and others in creating and sustaining healing environments. The potential impact of QCL on nurses and the healthcare workforce offers enhanced linkages between professional practice and job satisfaction, employee engagement, quality and safety outcomes, care experience scores, operational performance, retention, and team cohesion. The organization can further promote sustainable caring cultures through inclusion of QCL principles and expectations in role profiles, job descriptions, interview tools, orientation, 360-degree feedback processes, continuing education, professional governance structures, rewards and recognition programs, and employee benefits.

QUIZ QUESTIONS

1. Which statement best describes a unitary worldview?

    a) Relationships require time

    b) Environment is controlled

    c) Everything is connected

    d) Focus is service oriented

    Correct Answer: c

2. Separatist views found in leadership may include all the following except:

    a) Top-down decision making

    b) Focus on control

    c) Reductionist processes

    d) Change as a dynamic

    Correct Answer: d

3. Quantum worldview parallels the growing commitment of nursing scholars to unitary thinking for nursing phenomena.

    a) True

    b) False

    Correct Answer: a

4. Second quantum concepts of "non-locality" and "non-local consciousness" are best defined as:

    a) Both universe and communication can be non-local

    b) Consciousness is not confined to the brain

    c) Both a & b

    d) None of the above

    Correct Answer: c

5. Healthcare leadership today is generally more unitary and evolved than Newtonian separatist or otherwise outdated transactional leadership principles.

    a) True

    b) False

    Correct Answer: b

    Rationale: Because principles of healthcare leadership are still largely embedded with Newtonian separatist outdated principles.

6. Caring Science Theory seeks to sustain human caring-healing and love, through:

   a) Knowledgeable and compassionate service to humankind

   b) Enhanced value for nursing care through evidence and metrics

   c) Caritas Processes that offer a checklist for creating caring relationships

   d) Advanced service-oriented models with theory-guided caring moments

   Correct Answer: a

7. New patterns of Quantum Caring Leadership principles offer directions for fixing broken systems through improved caregiver engagement and accountability.

   a) True

   b) False

   Correct Answer: b

   Rationale: Because new patterns of Quantum Caring Leadership principles offer directions for whole person-whole system, caring healing, and global healthcare organizations.

8. The congruence that unites quantum and caring leadership helps advance:

   a) Newtonian and transactional leadership tactics

   b) Distinct disciplinary foundations for new leadership practices and principles

   c) Innovative perspectives to manage operational efficiency and performance

   d) Established healthcare leadership theory, knowledge, and practices

   Correct Answer: b

9. An evolved Quantum Caring Leadership model invites new leadership thinking, critique, and consciousness for all healthcare leadership.

   a) True

   b) False

   Correct Answer: a

10. As Caring Science knowledge evolves toward the integration of "second quantum revolution" science, it aligns to Quantum Leadership ethics and principles that support a nursing specific leadership model.

    a) True

    b) False

    Correct Answer: b

    Rationale: Because Caring Science has evolved more explicitly, underpinned by "second quantum revolution" science and Quantum Leadership principles.

10

CARING SCIENCE–INFORMED LEADERSHIP

REFLECTIVE QUESTIONS

1. How is Caritas Leadership visible in your practice? What more can you do?

   Answer: Students need to share their observation, what they learned about Caritas Leadership in this chapter, and how they plan to respond in light of this learning.

2. What distinguishes Caritas/Caring Science–informed leadership from conventional patterns of leadership?

   Answer: Caring Science–informed leadership is guided by a distinct disciplinary foundation of nursing: a humanistic Unitary Philosophy; an Ethic of Equity-Belonging; a Relational Ontology; an expanded inner-Knowing/Epistemology; Caritas Literacy Language; Authentic Praxis of Being/Becoming.

3. How do Caritas leaders create a caring, healing environment?

   Answer: Caritas leaders create a caring, healing environment by engaging the heart, head, and hands as "the embodied, caring-loving consciousness engaged in informed, moral actions and practices."

4. Why is it essential for an academic Caritas leader to trust that people are able?

   Answer: Trusting that people are able honors and encourage people's capacities to be empathic, respectful, caring, compassionate, authentic, and willing and able to express their positive and negative feelings, as well as being able to speak to inequities and inequalities.

5.   How would you describe Caritas leaders in the academy?

     Answer: Caritas leaders lead with kindness, passion, humility, and engagement, listening, valuing, and trusting people to enable educational as well as organizational humanization for all—students, staff members, nurse educators, faculty, as well as managers.

ACTIVITY

Create a healing space for a group to gather in person or virtually. Engage in a centering exercise such as lighting a candle/flameless candle and intentional breathing awareness. Engage in any micro-practice that can create a safe space for participants (e.g., inspirational reading).

In a group circle format of two or more, reflect on your individual, current nursing leadership experiences and invite participants to share how they are integrating and/or how they can begin to integrate Caring Science–informed leadership practices.

Response to activity: Give each participant the opportunity to reflect and lovingly share their individual stories, experiences, and suggestions for integration. Suggest each participant commit to integrating one Caritas Leadership practice in the next week and share it back with the group.

Additional suggestions: Create a word cloud with the practices identified and share with each participant as a visual reminder of their commitment to Caritas Leadership.

QUIZ QUESTIONS

1.   Caritas leaders consider caring as a moral imperative to act ethically and justly.

     a) True

     b) False

  Correct Answer: a

2.   Caring Leadership is a way of being, knowing, and doing that facilitates human flourishing for leaders, staff, students, and their organizations.

     a) True

     b) False

  Correct Answer: a

3.   A caring, healing environment is experienced by nurse leaders as "the disconnected, illiterate unconscious actions and practices from a dehumanizing organization."

     a) True

     b) False

  Correct Answer: b

4. Caritas leaders consider all actors' perceptions and past experiences and their meanings to collaboratively engage and commit to the leader's vision regarding the transformation's insight.

    a) True

    b) False

    Correct Answer: b

5. Caritas leaders were invited to know themselves and others as caring persons to "seek new solutions" to challenges, difficulties, and problems from a Caring Science perspective.

    a) True

    b) False

    Correct Answer: a

6. The ontology of Caritas Leadership literacy begins and ends with self and invites leaders to:

    a) Form (versus deform)

    b) Guide the human creative spirit, away from the outer patterned, non-relational system-cultures (dyspraxis)

    c) Reconstruct, drawing upon inner subjective, creative life force of self/other in relation—co-creating Caritas ontological eupraxis as foundation for Caring Science Leadership

    d) All the above

    Correct Answer: d

7. Caritas leaders in acute care settings engage their hearts by engaging in which of these practices?

    a) Caring hiring practices, annual performance evaluations, and self-care practice interventions.

    b) Coaching and mentoring relationships, and strategic goal integration.

    c) Self-care micro practices, authentic presence, and mindful listening.

    d) Providing comfort measures, psychological safety, privacy, and aesthetic surroundings.

    Correct Answer: c

8. Which Caritas Process is not identified as a building block for Caritas Leadership practice in acute care settings?

    a) Caritas Process #3: Transpersonal presence; cultivating own spiritual practices

    b) Caritas Process #5: Authentically listening to another person's story

    c) Caritas Process #6: Creatively problem-solving—"solution-seeking"; creative use of self and all ways of knowing/being/doing/becoming

    d) Caritas Process #10: Open to spiritual, mystery, unknowns—allowing for miracles

    Correct Answer: d

9. Which answer does not pertain to Caritas Leadership in the academy?

   a) Caritas Leadership is grounded on a relational ontology and embraces collaboration.

   b) Caritas Leadership is crucial to advance nursing as both a discipline and a profession.

   c) Caritas leaders have a vision and already know what is best for the people they lead.

   d) Caritas leaders are social activists, inspiring, collaborating, sojourning with others—students, nurse educators, professors, administrators, community, government, and decision-makers.

Correct Answer: c

10. Which answer is the most accurate?

   a) Caritas leaders embrace equity.

   b) Caritas leaders advocate for others to develop their voice.

   c) Caritas leaders create opportunities for others to claim their power.

   d) All the answers above are accurate.

Correct Answer: d

11

PROMOTING EXCEPTIONAL PATIENT EXPERIENCE THROUGH COMPASSIONATE CONNECTED CARE®

REFLECTIVE QUESTIONS

1. What is an important distinction between empathy and compassion?

   Answer: Empathy is the ability to deeply understand another's experience. It is an essential skill in creating a strong human connection with another person. Compassion includes the desire to do something to help another person who is suffering. Compassion creates the opportunity to intervene to reduce another person's suffering.

2. Why are patient experience surveys important to patient care?

   Answer: Patient experience surveys bring the patient voice into patient care. It is difficult to improve patient experience if we don't know where to focus our efforts. Robust and validated patient experience surveys provide actionable data to caregivers and leaders so they can focus improvement efforts in response to patient concerns.

3. How can practicing the 56-second connection improve patient care?

   Answer: Research has shown that human connection can be established in less than a minute. Utilizing this approach (see video in resource section), caregivers can apply the 56-second connection to any patient encounter.

4. Why is expert-level AI important to analyze patients' words reflecting their care experiences?

    Answer: Expert-level AI in a specific domain of discourse, such as patient experience, provides the analytical capabilities of a highly trained expert (human) analyst at scale. Just like a human analyst of narrative data, expert-level AI would identify the different meanings of the word "cool" in a comment like, "The temperature in my room was too cool" versus the same word in a comment like, "My nurse was cool." It is important for AI to detect such differences in meaning in patients' words about care experiences in order for us to accurately and reliably hear the voices of patients.

5. How does AI make it possible to create a narrative evidence basis for human caring?

    Answer: AI allows us to hear what patients say in large volumes and shows aggregate trends from patients' own words. With this capability, we gain empirical insights—based on narrative evidence—into what patients need and expect of human caregiving.

NARRATIVE

Community General Hospital is experiencing downward trending over the past two years for both patient experience and caregiver engagement scores. Organizational annual goals have included targets for selected patient experience, key performance indicators such as nurse communication scores and likelihood to recommend the hospital, and intent to leave the organization as a global measure of workforce engagement. Leaders used a number of tactical approaches to improve both engagement and patient experience scores. While efforts have sometimes resulted in temporary improvement, these gains do not last. Staff and leaders are frustrated as they are working hard to provide good patient care and to engage and support staff and caregivers.

How might they change their improvement approach to achieve success?

RESPONSE TO THE NARRATIVE

Validated patient and workforce surveys provide patients and staff with invaluable and actionable information if a robust data management strategy is employed. A strategic improvement approach has several key components. Quantitative data alone does not provide leaders with all the information they need to be successful. Qualitative data provides additional detail that can help to focus and refine improvement efforts. Qualitative data can be obtained through manual or AI-generated survey comment analysis, during leader rounding (on both patients and staff), and during staff town hall meetings or patient family advisory council meetings. Interventions or initiatives to improve patient experience and caregiver engagement must be based on the evidence and should be limited to two or three interventions. It is unrealistic to expect that leaders and staff can manage 10 or 15 improvement efforts at the same time with any degree of success, yet leaders report it is a common experience to be working on many initiatives at once. For example, leader rounding on staff and patients, hourly rounding, and bedside shift report are present to some degree in almost every healthcare organization in the US Press Ganey data show that these interventions are highly effective at improving patient experience, and leader rounds on staff at improving engagement, when done consistently and reliably. However, to maximize impact of these interventions, leaders must also focus on how rounds and bedside shift are done. Ensuring that leaders and caregivers embed learned behaviors that convey empathy, caring, and compassion into patient and staff encounters is just as important as implementing evidence-based interventions consistently and reliably. The Compassionate Connected Care model can provide organizations with an action framework to build on their own caring model to advance and operationalize it in their own organizations.

QUIZ QUESTIONS

1. Compassion and empathy are interchangeable terms.

    a) True

    b) False

    Correct Answer: b

2. Empathy can be learned.

    a) True

    b) False

    Correct Answer: a

3. The Compassionate Connected Care model for the patient includes which of the following domains?

    a) Caring

    b) Operational

    c) Clinical

    d) All the above

    Correct Answer: d

4. Caregivers may also experience suffering.

    a) True

    b) False

    Correct Answer: a

5. Which of the following outcomes are impacted by using an empathic, patient-centered approach to care?

    a) Patient experience scores

    b) Caregiver engagement scores

    c) Both a & b

    d) Neither a nor b

    Correct Answer: c

6. AI analysis of narrative data should include:

    a) Sentiment analysis

    b) Categorization

    c) Both a & b

    d) Neither a nor b

Correct Answer: c

7. What did Clavelle et al.'s (2019) study identify as the top theme of extraordinary nursing care in their AI analysis of patients' comments about excellent nurses?

    a) Professionalism

    b) Punctuality

    c) Courtesy & respect

    d) Skill & knowledge

Correct Answer: c

8. The larger the number of distinct insights that AI can extract per comment, the better it can identify the root causes behind patients' positive or negative experiences.

    a) True

    b) False

Correct Answer: a

9. Ideally, for expert-level AI, the unit of analysis for sentiment and categorization should be a:

    a) Sentence

    b) Phrase

    c) Section

    d) Paragraph

Correct Answer: b

10. By allowing us to hear what patients say in large volumes, AI makes it possible to create a _____ for the science and practice of human caring.

    a) Pedagogical model

    b) Specific formula

    c) Different language

    d) Narrative evidence basis

Correct Answer: d

12

APPLYING COMPLEXITY SCIENCE IN PROMOTING COMMUNITY AND POPULATION HEALTH

REFLECTIVE QUESTIONS

1. From your knowledge and experience, how would you describe healthcare as a complex system and the relationship to complexity theory?

   Answer: Healthcare is a complex system with various regulations, policies, stakeholders, and payment systems. Complexity science refers to systems with many components, interconnections, and unpredictability, which can also describe healthcare.

2. Describe population and community health as a complex adaptive system from a nurse leader's perspective as described in this chapter.

   Answer: Population and community health is a complex adaptive system (CAS) with open boundaries, multiple levels, control constraints, adaptation, and non-linear causality boundaries. Nurse leaders need to recognize the characteristics of CAS and create an adaptive space for organizations and team members to perform creatively and innovatively.

3. Describe global threats and/or disaster examples that can benefit from complexity leadership as described in this chapter.

   Answer: Nurses globally are learning extensively how to deal rapidly with multiple, complex issues during disasters such as a global pandemic, fires in Australia, the tsunami and nuclear reactor leak in Japan, earthquakes in Haiti, and increased terrorism attacks on innocent citizens.

In addition, poverty is increasing, and more vulnerable and marginalized communities around the world are without affordable healthcare.

4. Identify at least two actions suggested in the chapter to assist with skill acquisition or increased participation in population health initiatives or health policy development.

    Answer:

    Example 1—Volunteer or seek governance roles in a hospital setting or community initiative, such as conducting a community health assessment.

    Example 2—Participate in working with vulnerable populations as it relates to social determinants of health (safe neighborhood project, public education initiatives, clean water, or building healthy food markets).

    Example 3—Explore working with government elected officials on an issue of personal interest.

    Example 4—Promote sharing clinical experiences with other clinicians, researchers, and policy makers to drive new policy changes.

5. What is at least one resource you can utilize from this chapter to assist you with conducting health policy assessments and foster your participation in health policy development?

    Answer:

    The Centers for Disease Control and Prevention (CDC) Policy Process Framework to conduct policy analysis. This framework can define or assess the problem, identify potential policy solutions, analyze, and prioritize the best solution for adoption and evaluation (https://www.cdc.gov/policy/analysis/process).

    CDC Policy Analysis Key Questions for implementing policy. This document could be an effective worksheet in the assessment Policy Analysis: Key Questions (cdc.gov).

NARRATIVE

The Chief Nursing Officer, Senior Charge Nurse, and staff nurses of the obstetric department in a Chinese children's hospital collaborated with a US nurse scientist in a research project in Qingdao, China (Yu et al., 2021). The nursing team identified the breastfeeding rate (17.9%) in their hospital was much lower than the national rate in China (23%), which is a work in progress toward the World Health Organization goal of 50% by 2025 (WHO, 2018). Utilizing project data, the exclusive breastfeeding rate of premature infants was 1.8% and contributed to the separation between mothers and premature infants who were admitted to the Newborn Intensive Care Unit (NICU). From a population health perspective, the team understood, breastfeeding is associated with decreased risk for many early-life diseases and conditions, such as otitis media, respiratory tract infections, asthma, and sudden infant death syndrome. The project team identified gaps between best practice and current practice and the components involved in breastfeeding NICU newborns. From a complex adaptive system perspective and process review, interviews with 17 staff nurses revealed a lack of breastmilk storage equipment in the unit. Interviews with 70 mothers demonstrated they had limited visitation time which restricted their breastfeeding time in the NICU. These system components, relationships, and interconnections provided a better understanding of the issue's complexity and ultimately encouraged new ways of thinking and practices within this unit.

Innovative changes achieved increased education for nurses and mothers on breastfeeding; new processes led to new governance (policies); and improved health outcomes are yielding an improvement in breastfeeding among premature newborns rates from 17.9% to 52.7% (exceeding the WHO goal of 50%), and the exclusive breastfeeding rates from 1.8% to 4.1% over a three-year period. In addition, this case demonstrated international nurses collaborating in critical research, which improved health outcomes.

Yu, G., Liu, F., Zhao, Y., Kong, Y., & Wei, H., (2021). Promoting breastfeeding and lactation among mothers of premature newborns in a hospital in China. *Nursing for Women's Health, 25*(1), 21–29. https://doi.org/10.1016/j.nwh.2020.11.005.

RESPONSE TO THE NARRATIVE

1. Please explain the nurses' roles in promoting population health in this case.

   Answer: From this example, you can see how nurses' expertise and experience can make a difference, and how a population health focus can be implemented in medical and nursing care in the form of prevention in a hospital NICU setting (breastfeeding benefits to prevent early-life diseases and conditions).

2. How did systems thinking operationalize changes in this clinical setting?

   Answer: From this example, nurses led changes to enhance nurse education. Breastfeeding was one example of improving NICU newborn breastfeeding rates, thus improving patient outcomes (NICU breastfeeding rates).

3. Explain how CAS thinking determined several needed changes to enhance NICU breastfeeding rates.

   Answer: From this example, the "complex" part of CAS refers to the vast interconnectedness of these systems, such as care of a NICU newborn, and the many processes involved in the criticality of the medical care and ensuring there is adequate equipment (e.g., breastmilk storage equipment in this case).

QUIZ QUESTIONS

1. A complex adaptive system has the following characteristics _____.

   a) Distributed control

   b) Connectivity

   c) Co-evolution

   d) Emergent order

   e) All above

   Correct Answer: e

2. Historically, healthcare organizations operate as a manufactory and machinery, with strict hierarchical power, rules, and assembly lines.

    a) True

    b) False

Correct Answer: a

3. The traditional rigid and hierarchical organizational structures offer the structure and flexibility needed for production, innovation, and creation.

    a) True

    b) False

Correct Answer: b

4. Population and community health requires _____.

    a) A clear-cut strategy to improve effectiveness

    b) A hierarchical structure to allow high productivity

    c) Global connection and collaboration to promote population health

    d) Everyone working independently to ensure efficiency

Correct Answer: c

5. A great facilitator granting legitimacy in global and population health is _____.

    a) The friend relationship with influential leaders

    b) A dynamic policy process with minimum specifications

    c) A precise rule-following policy

    d) The continuation of the current protocol

Correct Answer: b

6. Nurses are a major healthcare workforce and can work most effectively within the profession.

    a) True

    b) False

Correct Answer: b

7. The dynamic and collaborative process of population management lends itself to complexity science and involves the basic principles, including _____.

    a) Adaptiveness

    b) Emergency

    c) Non-linearity

    d) Connectivity

    e) All the above

Correct Answer: e

8. In disaster management and building the social infrastructure of adaptive response, intervention strategies at the macro-level can promote population health and community resilience.

   a) True

   b) False

   Correct Answer: b

9. During a global population threat, such as COVID-19, the nursing profession functions at its best if nurses take the following actions except_____:

   a) Be aware of health policies at the global level

   b) Be aware of government policies

   c) Pay close attention only to the local community

   d) Be involved in policy advocacy

   Correct Answer: c

10. In the US Public Health Service, government actions include _____.

    a) Public health surveillance of disease

    b) Free health access for the poor and elderly

    c) Evaluation of health promotion programs

    d) Research and education

    e) All the above

    Correct Answer: e

ASSEMBLING A UNIFYING FORCE: INTERPROFESSIONAL COLLABORATION TO IMPROVE HEALTHCARE

REFLECTIVE QUESTIONS

1. Eisler and Potter (2014) applied cultural transformation theory to healthcare systems and described how those systems fall along a continuum from domination- to partnership-based systems. List characteristics specific to a domination-based system.

    Answer: Domination systems include characteristics such as: rigid ranking, uni-directional communication (typically top-down), shame, blame, and fear.

2. List characteristics specific to a partnership-based system.

    Answer: Partnership systems include characteristics such as: mutual respect, bidirectional communication flows, individuals uplifting one another to act to their full potential, and an environment where individuals collaborate to work together towards a common goal.

3. Consider how a domination system impacts the patient experience within healthcare environments. Read the following example and then answer the question.

    Emely was 5. She and her mother, Lydia, were scared. Emely was admitted to the hospital for chronic leg pain, and they both had a lot of questions. As a non-native English speaker, Lydia did the best she could to understand the nurses and physicians when they told her that Emely would have labs done, various tests, and possible treatments. The healthcare team made little attempt to ensure that Lydia understood what they were saying, and rarely included her in any decisions. She continued to ask questions and seek partnership from the team during the journey but didn't even know what questions to ask. Behind closed doors, the physicians discussed the cancer diagnosis and asked that the nurses not discuss it with the family. They withheld the information for four days. On a Friday afternoon, the healthcare team took 10 minutes to tell Lydia that Emely was diagnosed with cancer. Lydia was alone in the room with Emely; no support persons were present. She was left with more questions than she initially had and felt too rushed to ask anything. Whom could she turn to about her fears when so far no one had made the effort to listen, to work in partnership, to truly care for them? Lydia and Emely felt alone.

List some ways in which the healthcare team exhibited domination characteristics during the care of Lydia and Emely.

Answer:

a) Not involving Lydia and Emely in care

b) Withholding critical healthcare information from the patient and her mother

c) Lack of consideration of patient and mother's needs (family present, interpreter, time to ask questions) to ensure a safe environment

4. Read the following example from a partnership-based perspective and then answer the following questions:

Emely was 5. She and her mother, Lydia, were scared. Emely was admitted to the hospital for chronic leg pain, and they both had a lot of questions. The healthcare team immediately recognized the need for an interpreter and arranged one to be present as they discussed with Lydia all the labs that could be done, various tests, and possible treatments. They asked her if she needed other resources or support during this time. Lydia and Emely discussed their fears with the healthcare team. Each day the healthcare team would discuss any new information or change in plans, including them in all the decisions. Once they identified that it was in fact cancer, the healthcare team held a meeting to discuss the information with Lydia as her family surrounded her. They supported Lydia as she asked her questions and provided her with resources in case more questions came up afterwards. Lydia and Emely knew they could turn to their healthcare team at any time with their fears and questions as the team had made every effort to listen, to work in partnership, and to truly care for them. Lydia and Emely felt safe.

List some ways in which the healthcare team exhibited partnership-based characteristics during the care of Lydia and Emely.

Answer:

a) Supporting Emely and Lydia to ensure their voice is present and heard (interpreter, space to ask questions)

b) Asking Emely and Lydia what resources or support they needed (instead of assuming)

c) Ensuring transparency in healthcare information (diagnosis, options)

5. How can partnership-based systems be used to transform healthcare at the bedside, in communities, across nations, and even the health of the planet?

     Answer: As demonstrated in the example above, partnership-based systems allow healthcare providers to ensure a safe environment for healing where the patient, their family, and the healthcare providers work together towards a common goal. Incorporating the characteristics of partnership-based systems breaks down the hierarchy, shame, and fear, replacing them with respect, innovation, and engagement. If, as a system, we uplift each other and collaborate towards a common goal, together we can create lasting change to improve health across the spectrum.

NARRATIVE

You are the Director of Public Health for a county in Northern California. Climate change is causing frequent and severe heat waves with high temperatures throughout the day and very little relief in the evenings. You are aware of numerous families living in older apartment buildings without air-conditioning and their indoor temperatures are continuing to rise. In addition, heavy winter snows led to massive growth of brush which has now dried and is fueling predictions that this will be a very severe fire year.

You are aware that your county has an aging population with many chronic health issues. In addition to wildfires and severe heat, fires bring days with unhealthy air quality, which can be especially dangerous for people with asthma and other chronic lung diseases.

Climate change impacts the health of populations, but it also impacts the health of individuals. Recently one of the county's visiting nurses raised a concern about an insulin dependent diabetic. The packaging for the insulin says "keep it at room temperature of 20-25°C (68-77°F) after opening. DO NOT store in the refrigerator." Without air-conditioning, indoor temperatures are no longer less than 77 degrees. Is this patient safe?

RESPONSE TO THE NARRATIVE

1. Make a list of the actual and potential health issues in this scenario. Define "health" broadly using a planetary health lens.

     Answer:

     a) Heat episodes without adequate cooling, posing threats to the health of vulnerable people.

     b) Potentially severe wildfires with poor air quality and the need to stay indoors with windows closed.

     c) Impacts that high home heat can have on medications and other aspects of the treatment plan.

     d) None of the problems in this scenario can be solved by one discipline working in a silo.

2. Choose one health problem and address the following questions:

    a) When forming an interprofessional team to address this problem, which health professions need to be included?

    Answer: Public health and ambulatory nurses, physicians and advanced practice nurses, emergency department staff, social workers, chronic disease specialists such as cardiologists and pulmonologists, and community health workers should be included.

    b) When forming a transdisciplinary team to address this problem, which disciplines and stakeholders need to be included?

    Answer: In addition to the above health professionals, add schoolteachers, managers of cooling shelters, places of faith, community centers, and first responders such as EMTs and firefighters.

    c) You know that it is essential for all ideas and all voices to be heard if the teams are to create the transformative changes that are necessary. List two group norms that you can suggest, encouraging teams to work in partnership rather than hierarchies of domination.

    Answer:

        i) Everyone's contributions are valuable.

        ii) Use a "lean in-lean out" strategy during group discussions. If you have already spoken, lean back to let others speak; if you have not spoken, lean in and share your insights.

QUIZ QUESTIONS

1. In 1972, the Institute of Medicine (IOM) issued the first report proposing that high-quality care for patients living with chronic illness requires a team approach.

        a) True

        b) False

    Correct Answer: a

2. Leaders in partnership-based systems are appointed based on ranking rather than expertise.

        a) True

        b) False

    Correct Answer: b

3. Key factors required for interprofessional practice include the following: (Mark all that apply)

    a) Understanding that each discipline makes a unique contribution to the team

    b) Understanding the roles and responsibilities of each profession

    c) Team members need to share the same physical space for interprofessional collaboration

    d) The nurse-physician dyad is the primary leadership nucleus of interprofessional care

    Correct Answer: a, b

4. Planetary health is described by the following statements: (Mark all that apply)

    a) The nursing profession recognizes that the environment is part of the healing paradigm

    b) Transdisciplinary research is needed to create effective solutions

    c) The primary purpose of planetary health is to address climate change

    d) The health of humans and the health of the planet are deeply interconnected

    Correct Answers: a, b, d

5. Global nursing leaders have collaborated in partnership to create Nurses Drawdown (NDD). Which of the following statements are correct? (Mark all that apply)

    a) NDD solutions focus on improving the health of the planet, not human health

    b) NDD teaches nurses about evidence-based solutions to drawdown greenhouse gases

    c) Nurses are encouraged to bring NDD solutions to patients, families, and communities

    Correct Answer: b, c

6. Cuban healthcare relies on a government-run public health system that, despite limited resources, has similar or better outcomes than other industrialized countries.

    a) True

    b) False

    Correct Answer: a

7. The following statements describe the Cuban healthcare system: (Select all that apply)

    a) Consultorios offer primary care delivered by collaborative teams in neighborhood settings. These teams provide care for up to 700-1,500 residents in their area

    b) The Cuban healthcare model can easily be transferred to any country and be effective

    c) There is a focus on the health of the community through disease prevention and wellness education

    d) Polyclinicas form the second tier of the Cuban healthcare system and provide more advanced specialty care

    e) Cuba's public health success is based on ample healthcare and economic resources

    Correct Answers: a, c, d

8. An interprofessional education offering is defined as an activity where a minimum of four or more healthcare professionals learn with, from, and about each other with a focus on improving collaboration and quality of care.

    a) True

    b) False

Correct Answer: b

9. Health professionals contribute informally to collaboration with each other by three essential actions: bridging professional and social gaps between each other, negotiating overlapping roles and tasks, and creating spaces to be able to work effectively in teams.

    a) True

    b) False

Correct Answer: a

10. The following are examples of interprofessional collaborative practice: (Mark all that apply)

    a) Leadership is based on rank and use of top-down communication flow

    b) Interprofessional collaborative teams that use telehealth for care conferences

    c) Team-based community clinic care of a patient with multiple psychosocial needs

    d) Complex care for acutely ill patients in the hospital setting

    e) The role of nurses is to support physician-led teams

Correct Answers: b, c, d

LEADERSHIP IN DISASTER PREPAREDNESS AND RESPONSE

REFLECTIVE QUESTIONS

1. Why do disaster nurses need to minimize personal and moral conflicts that may occur in disaster response and recovery?

   Answer: The leading conflict involves the struggle between taking care of family and wanting to help the community. It is essential that nurses prepare for themselves and their families first, including emergency supplies and a reunification plan, and then deploy to help the community. We need disaster personnel to be able to focus on the mission without distractions due to a lack of family preparation.

2. During disaster response and recovery, nurses may be asked by the Incident Commander (IC) to be a part of a non-healthcare-related disaster team or asked to complete tasks that are not nursing-related, such as debris removal or food distribution. How should nurse leaders respond to these requests and the potential implications of both accepting and declining the assignment?

   Answer: The IC is considered the authority for deployment, and in general, team members need to act based on the IC's orders/plan. Nurses may not be needed to provide nursing care but can be essential to a cleanup team or another essential task. For example, ensuring people have water, food, and safety is paramount, and nurses can be part of any team when needed. We do what needs to be done, and only the IC has the whole picture. The IC should not give orders that are unsafe, unethical, or illegal—if you are asked to complete something you consider to be unethical, illegal, or unsafe, you should discuss this with the team leader, who will then present the concern to the IC. The chain of command and organization of communication and actions is critical in disaster response.

3. Discuss vulnerable populations and special considerations nurse leaders must include in disaster preparation, mitigation, response, and recovery.

   Answer: Each community is different, so this is an individual response. Potential considerations include accommodations for persons with physical or emotional limitations, the elderly, children, and those without permanent residences. Nursing homes and group homes need to be included in the community assessment and disaster planning. Nurses need to know where the vulnerable elderly reside and be aware of available resources to assist. We must include medical equipment considerations in our disaster planning. For example, a person who lives alone, does not drive, and is on oxygen would be very vulnerable to power outages and flooding. Encourage families to be involved in proactive decision-making instead of waiting until disasters strike. Public service announcements and the involvement of key community groups to spread disaster preparation information could be an effective way to help others prepare for disasters.

4. Community members have many spiritual, cultural, and ethnic differences. Considering your community population and their ethnic and cultural differences, how would you plan for these differences in the disaster preparation process?

   Answer: Each community is different, so this is an individual response. Potential considerations include accommodations for persons with limitations, the elderly, children, those without permanent residences, and various cultural and religious groups. For example, a religious group may need opportunities to worship and pray during the day. Some may have special dietary considerations. Some may speak different languages and need interpreters. In all situations, we must be sensitive to the individual needs of our community members and complete community assessments as part of the disaster preparation phase to ensure we are prepared for the special needs of our people.

5. What are your community's strengths and resources for disaster preparation? What are key challenges and mitigation measures to address those challenges?

   Answer: Each community is different, so this question asks participants to really look at their community. Each county in the US should have a community assessment that can include valuable information. Strengths may include the healthcare system with a trauma center, paramedics on the paid emergency response teams, a full/paid fire and rescue department, sound schools to use as shelters, easy access into and out of the area, etc. Challenges may relate to many of the same areas, such as an all-volunteer fire and rescue, lack of safe buildings for shelters, proximity to a river that tends to flood, densely populated areas, or areas in which people are spread out by miles, etc. Challenge students to dig into their community and recognize what they can contribute to the health and well-being of their community through their nursing leadership.

ACTIVITY

Assign students to small groups of four to five students considering the diversity and different learning styles of students. Ask students to review the scenario below and then identify the resources needed to respond to the disaster effectively. Each student will assume a different incident command leadership role based on the community needs they identify and present their request for resources based on what they believe is necessary to safely assist their community.

Scenario: Emerald Place is a small, quaint coastal community with a population of 3,000 people that enjoys tourists from all over the world in the summer months. During the summer months, the population increases to over 10,000, including visitors. The town has a popular waterfront area, which sits at sea level, with many locally owned retail shops that sell local crafts, clothing, coffee, and baked goods, along with several excellent seafood restaurants. Tourists enjoy staying at the many bed and breakfasts and historic homes rented through online rental websites. The town has a mayor, five town commissioners, a town manager, and support staff. They have combined police, fire, and rescue department with eight police officers, 10 paid firefighters with two fire trucks, and two rescue squads manned with emergency medical technicians. The electricity is operated by a large corporation located four hours away. The town has a district public water plant that supplies 90% of the population. The remaining 10% have personal wells. There is one main internet provider that services the area. There are three schools: one elementary, one middle, and one high school. The nearest hospital is 30 miles away in a larger city. There are two primary healthcare offices, two pharmacies, and one dentist in the town. There are two grocery stores, one locally owned hardware store, and a lumber store. Most local residents travel to other towns to work, with a 30-mile commute at a minimum. The local population is predominately English-speaking, with 50% of the residents under the age of 65.

On August 20th, a hurricane has formed in the Atlantic Ocean. As the storm nears, it strengthens. The projected path is within 50 miles of Emerald Place, with anticipated landfall in 96 hours. Based on the information provided, you are responsible for forming a disaster response team and making initial preparations.

Here are some questions to consider:

1.   What are the hazards, threats, and risks?

2.   Who would you need on your team?

3.   What resources do you need?

4.   What are the concerns you identify that would need to be addressed?

5.   What are the priorities for the disaster management team?

RESPONSE TO THE ACTIVITY

Students will need to first recognize the potential hazards, risks, and threats. The town is at sea level, so flooding of the waterfront affecting the businesses is a significant threat. Since it is summer, many international tourists are in the town, which increases the complexity of response efforts by increasing the number and the diversity of people. Cultural and language barriers may impact preparation, response, and recovery. Since this threat is a hurricane, wind and rain damage to property and essential utilities can be expected, disrupting the town's essential functions.

Key team members would be the emergency operations director, the mayor, emergency services (police/fire/rescue squad) representative, school representative, public information representative, and public health/healthcare representative at a minimum.

Key actions would include evacuation in an orderly fashion, identification of locations for emergency shelters, developing a list of needed supplies (including water, non-perishable food, tarps, rope, tools such as hammers/nails, first aid supplies, blankets), and agencies that need to be contacted/added to the plan including American Red Cross, larger nearby community mutual aid, and National Guard request to the state at a minimum. Priorities include communicating the threat to the public in a way to avoid panic and prompt them to take action to prepare, including evacuation arrangements to move to shelters as the storm approaches. We want the community to respond calmly and take care of themselves as much as possible, prepared to be without electricity, internet, and water services indefinitely. Windows need to be boarded, non-essential services need to be suspended, and an "all hands on deck" call needs to be publicized, helping in the mobilization prior to the storm's impact.

QUIZ QUESTIONS

1. When determining if an event qualifies as a disaster, the key determinant is the size of the event.

    a) True

    b) False

    Correct Answer: b

    Rationale: Disasters are not determined by the size of the event but rather by the magnitude of the impact on the community that exceeds the current response capacity.

2. Disaster management is proactive in planning and reactive, when necessary, as all potential threats and hazards cannot be reasonably anticipated.

    a) True

    b) False

    Correct Answer: a

    Rationale: While all disasters cannot be determined, the various main threats and hazards can be assessed with proactive planning to address the most likely scenarios. We plan for the worst while we hope for the best.

3. All community members must be accepted into disaster emergency shelters regardless of their medical conditions.

    a) True

    b) False

Correct Answer: b

Rationale: Shelters are set up based on expected needs and have different levels. Not all shelters can accept residents with medical needs and disabilities, which require a higher level of care and medical capabilities.

4. Nurses are licensed to practice in any state where a formal disaster declaration has been made.

    a) True

    b) False

Correct Answer: b

Rationale: Nurses who volunteer for disaster response and recovery must maintain the same nursing practice standards and ethical responsibilities, focusing on doing no harm and the greater good for all those affected by the disaster.

5. Church facilities or community buildings may be used to meet temporary housing needs for medically fragile residents.

    a) True

    b) False

Correct Answer: a

Rationale: The type of facility is irrelevant if the facility has the capability to meet those needs.

6. The primary goals of disaster management include which of the following:

    a) Reduce loss of life

    b) Minimize property damage

    c) Minimize environmental damage

    d) All the above

Correct Answer: d

7. A well-developed disaster plan will include the key missions listed below except which of the following?

>   a) Prevention
>
>   b) Protection
>
>   c) Mitigation
>
>   d) Communication
>
>   e) Recovery

Correct Answer: d

Rationale: Communication is not a key mission of disaster planning but a vital component in all mission areas.

8. Extreme cold temperatures have been predicted in a community, and authorization by the county health director has been given to open a warming shelter from sundown to sunrise for the following three nights. Which level of nursing response is required to assist?

>   a) Level I—Basic RN education
>
>   b) Level II—Some specialized education in disaster management
>
>   c) Level III—Advanced education in disaster management
>
>   d) None of the above—nurses do not need to be involved

Correct Answer: c

9. Personal causes of psychological distress which may manifest during a disaster include:

>   a) Lack of electricity impacting communication efforts
>
>   b) Lack of cash on hand for purchases of food, supplies, and medications
>
>   c) Misinformation from social media on available resources
>
>   d) All the above

Correct Answer: d

10. This part of disaster planning involves health surveillance aimed at tracking communicable diseases, health risks, and subsequent chronic diseases. Select the best answer.

>   a) Continuity of Operations Plan
>
>   b) Geographic Information System
>
>   c) Disaster Epidemiology
>
>   d) National Incident Management System

Correct Answer: c

15

NURSING LEADERSHIP IN THE GLOBAL HEALTH CONTEXT

REFLECTIVE QUESTIONS

1. Please discuss why it is important for nurse leaders to understand the macro-level implications of policies.

   Answer: Larger cultural, social, and economic consequences often exacerbate the poor health outcomes that often affect the most vulnerable in society. Macro-level factors are often the "big picture" or systemic structures that influence facets of care. For example, we may see that a patient is labeled "noncompliant" or is frequently readmitted to a hospital with the same diagnosis. Do we as nurses understand what may be genuinely going on with a patient or choose to label them as such? For instance, do we understand or consider the underlying factors that may force a patient to be "noncompliant?" Could it be they do not make enough money to pay for medications in addition to other expenses such as housing, food, and transportation? Or do they live very far from a pharmacy to be able to get their medication? Or do they have reliable transportation to be able to purchase healthy, affordable food options? All these factors are the macro-level or systemic concerns that in turn affect patient health and outcomes.

2. How does Rao and Kelleher's (2005) gender-specific framework offer insight into empowering women and transforming change across societies?

   Answer: It's a two-pronged approach, which involves a shift in consciousness and engagement with culturally normative beliefs. This second phase goes beyond an individual level and examines society and commonly held assumptions that undergird gendered inequalities. This is a reflective process to investigate beliefs that oneself and others take for granted critically. This refined understanding informs the analysis on what needs to change and how society can be a part of that change process.

3.   What are three characteristics that would be needed of a globally minded nursing and midwifery leader?

Answer:

   a) Adaptability and innovation: The profession is changing due to technology, globalization, the nursing shortage, and the aging population. Nursing leaders need to think creatively about how the profession's landscape will survive and thrive for the next 100 years.

   b) Policy orientation: Thinking about how politics and governance structures influence and impact the profession

   c) Sensitivity to contextual diversity: Keeping patients at the center but also considering the needs of the profession.

4.   Explain the importance or lack thereof of the nursing profession within global health governance.

Answer: Nurses make invaluable contributions to national and international health systems and are the gatekeepers of health systems due to their intimate involvement with every facet of care delivery. The lack of nursing perspectives is detrimental because they are missing from policy decisions that influence care delivery. Unfortunately, nurses are largely invisible in the global health governance landscape despite their impact. Nursing expertise needs to be better leveraged and harnessed to influence policy, service delivery, and ultimately the public's welfare.

5.   What are three ways nurses can increase their skill set in becoming more globally minded and politically conscious?

Answer:

   a) Reaching out to local legislators, offering their expertise on health or non-health-related issues

   b) Joining and becoming active in a professional organization

   c) Taking continuing education classes and courses geared toward leadership and policy development

ACTIVITY

Direct students to read the following scenario:

Scenario: Janet is a 28-year-old staff nurse who has been a nurse for six years. She has primarily worked in an acute care setting with older geriatric patients dealing with chronic diseases for most of her career. Recently she has become more interested in working internationally and relocating abroad to use her skill set in a different country. She has seen job postings for leadership and managerial positions with global health organizations. Still, she is not sure how to gain experience to be a viable candidate for those jobs. She does not have any experience working in global health but recently saw an advertisement for an international conference in her city and decided it might be a great way to network and meet people connected to and working in global health. This is Janet's first conference that is not specifically focused on her clinical expertise and not exclusively for nurses.

At the conference's networking social, she feels isolated, anxious, and inadequate since she does not have any global health experience and she does not know anyone at this event. But she also realizes this is an excellent opportunity as numerous international organizations with employment opportunities and major players in global health are in attendance.

Divide students into groups of four and have them go through the following exercise. Within each group, have the students assume the role of a first-time attendee at an international global health conference. Questions for students to consider:

1. How would you advise Janet to approach networking at this social?

2. How can Janet leverage and highlight her clinical expertise amongst a group of non-nurse clinicians?

3. How can Janet prepare for future conferences and networking opportunities to maximize her experience?

4. Reflect on how isolated Janet feels about not having many nursing colleagues around and being outside of her "comfort zone." What are ways to create a more inclusive environment within your own workplace, network, and organization?

RESPONSE TO THE ACTIVITY

1. How would you advise Janet to approach networking at this social?

    Answers:

    - Take a few breaths and relax. Janet should remember why she came and what she hoped to get out of the conference and networking event.

    - Survey the room for a friendly face or someone in attendance by themselves to approach as a first step.

    - Think of relevant conversation starters and introduce herself, asking things like:

        - Where are you from?

        - What interested you in (blank) conference?

        - Have you attended this before? What has been your favorite session or speaker?

        - Exit the conversation politely when she is finished.

- Exchange contact information if necessary.

- Repeat these steps with other people or organizational representatives that may be in attendance.

2. How can Janet leverage and highlight her clinical expertise among a group of non-nurse clinicians?

    Answer:

    - Janet can speak about her experiences and stories about care delivery and patient experiences. Many people who work in global health do not have the patient interaction or systems delivery acumen that Janet possesses as a bedside nurse.

    - She can also offer the provider's perspective and the challenges and opportunities presented in her work environment and how that may be similar and different in a global health setting.

3. How can Janet prepare for future conferences and networking opportunities to maximize her experience?

    Answer:

    - Review who will be in attendance ahead of time (via an abstract booklet, social media, etc.) to be intentional about the connections she wants to make.

    - Consider setting up meetings in advance with key contacts or organizations she wants to learn more about or has an interest in.

        - Introduce herself in an email and see if she could meet with them during a break in the conference or at a networking session.

    - Have a goal and objective in mind in what she intends to get out of the networking event or conference.

    - Bring business cards.

    - Have a schedule for herself to outline what she wants to see at the conference and which events, such as networking, she wants to attend.

    - Utilize social media to post about the conference or networking event using the #hashtag.

    - Follow up with people after the conference via email and/or social media (LinkedIn, etc.).

    - Read up on recent news or industry trends for the conference she is attending to be current and have talking points at networking events.

4. Reflect on how isolated Janet feels about not having many nursing colleagues around and being outside of her "comfort zone." What are ways to create a more inclusive environment within your own workplace, network, and organization?

    Answer:
    - Self-reflect on why you want to create a more inclusive network; make sure you are doing it for the right reasons.
    - Assess your current network and consider your own biases, stereotypes, and tendencies.
    - Look to make connections and build a positive relationship with new people you meet.
    - Improve listening skills.
    - Join social clubs outside your professional interests.
    - Leverage social media to reach out to people with both similar and dissimilar interests.
    - Step outside of your silo, whether that be in your professional or personal circles.
    - Utilize your existing network to make introductions.

    Organization specific:
    - Send a welcome email and offer to be a contact person to help new hires navigate their new role at your organization regardless of their title or position.
    - Join existing groups within your organization such as an employee resource group for broadening your network and potentially volunteering for events or leadership opportunities.

QUIZ QUESTIONS

1. Networking is an important tool to expand opportunities for nurses.

    a) True

    a) False

    Correct Answer: a

2. Which of the following will allow you to be better prepared for conferences and networking events?

    a) Bring business cards

    b) Utilize social media to post about the conference

    c) Have a goal when attending the conference

    d) All the above

    Correct Answer: d

3. Which of the following statements would not be a conversation starter at a conference or networking event?

> a) Where are you from?
>
> b) Have you attended the conference before?
>
> c) Can you offer me a job?
>
> d) What has been your favorite session thus far?

Correct Answer: c

4. Janet's bedside clinical experience would not be an asset when highlighting her clinical expertise.

> a) True
>
> b) False

Correct Answer: b

5. Email is an appropriate avenue to following up with contacts met at a conference.

> a) True
>
> b) False

Correct Answer: a

6. Self-reflection is an important aspect to consider before making your environments (work, professional, and personal) more inclusive.

> a) True
>
> b) False

Correct Answer: a

7. Which of the following could be a possible location to find a list of conference attendees to plan meetings and networking opportunities?

> a) Conference abstract
>
> b) Social media
>
> c) None of the above
>
> d) Both a and b

Correct Answer: d

8. Which of the following are ways to create a more inclusive environment within your network?

> a) Improve your listening skills
>
> b) Join social clubs outside your professional interests
>
> c) Utilize your existing network to make introductions
>
> d) Both a and c

Correct Answer: d

9. Which of the following statements exemplify Janet leveraging her clinical expertise at the global health conference?

    a) "I do not have any global health experience."

    b) "Although I am new to global health, I have had six years of experience caring for patients, working within a healthcare system, and I have a good understanding of the challenges of care delivery in an urban setting."

    c) "I came to this conference to learn about global health."

    d) "What qualifications are you looking for to hire people at your organization?"

    Correct Answer: b

10. Having a diverse network of personal contacts can be one effective strategy to increasing your professional connections.

    a) True

    b) False

    Correct Answer: a

16

HEALTHCARE LEADERSHIP IN PROMOTING THE USE OF EVIDENCE

REFLECTIVE QUESTIONS

1. What happens when leaders and clinicians conduct their roles without using the best evidence to inform their thinking and actions?

   Answer: Leaders and clinicians who do not conduct their roles using the best evidence to support their thinking and action will not achieve quality, safe patient outcomes. This is due to the fact that their actions could be guided by trial and error, and thus, the outcomes of their actions are unpredictable and not necessarily based on the highest set of evidence/standards. When this happens, substandard care and services are provided, and the opportunity for medical error leading to small to serious errors can occur.

2. Given what you learned from this chapter, how can healthcare systems better support their leaders and clinicians in the application of best evidence for their decisions and practice?

   Answer: Executive leaders in organizations must value the use of evidence and deem its use as critical as part of all role responsibilities for all leaders and staff. This means that financial, material, and human resources must be allocated to ensure that all four domains of evidence can be achieved in their setting. Leaders and staff must be supported in their efforts to be competent in how to discern, support, and often to use the four domains of evidence; provided an infrastructure that enables the use of evidence in their decision-making and actions; and recognized and rewarded for applying evidence in the performance of all their role responsibilities.

3. What would you identify as the first three actions that need to be taken by nurse managers so that they can effectively influence clinicians to use evidence-based practice in the clinical setting?

    Answer:

    a) Be able to discern the difference and requirements for the application of the four domains of evidence

    b) Achieve competency in the use of evidence in one's own practice

    c) Use one's leadership influence to create an environment that can effectively support the use of evidence by leaders and staff

4. What gets in the way of your own use of best evidence in your daily practice, and what steps can you take to remove these barriers?

    Answer: Time and available resources. Steps that can be taken to remove the barrier of time include not seeing the use of evidence as an option, but rather part of the way things should be done, thus ensuring policies, procedures, and standards are evidence-based. Procuring available resources can be achieved by using one's leadership influence with other leaders and staff through storytelling that provides evidence-based examples on how targeted outcomes and exemplary clinical outcomes can only be achieved when they are evidence-based.

5. What would quality, safe care look like if best evidence and processes were used consistently by leaders and staff?

    Answer: Patient care and services will be provided in such a way that targeted outcomes of intended outcomes upheld by safety and quality will consistently be achieved without preventable harm and variation.

NARRATIVE

In 2014, the department of nursing at Memorial Sloan Kettering (MSK), an ANCC Magnet designated and NCI designated comprehensive cancer center, underwent organizational changes at the executive nursing level. The Senior Vice President and Chief Nursing Officer (SVP CNO) reorganized the divisions of nursing practice, quality, and education under the newly created office of the Deputy Chief Nursing Officer (DCNO). One of the deliverables the DCNO was given was to create, launch, and sustain an evidence-based practice (EBP) infrastructure across the nursing enterprise. As an internationally recognized oncology nursing service, these leaders believed that applying evidence to nursing care delivery would ensure MSK's leadership position in oncology nursing practice. Using a high-reliability framework, the DCNO set out to strengthen the department's approach to EBP. Leadership commitment was foundational to the full actualization of the vision and to ensure sustained EBP competency for every nurse across the care continuum. A partnership with the Helene Fuld Health Trust National Institute for Evidence-based Practice (EBP) was put in motion to leverage an innovative, deliberate, and customized college-level EBP immersion for the nursing enterprise at MSK. At the outset, a pivotal decision was made by the DCNO: all nursing leadership, inclusive of CNO, DCNO, Nursing Directors, Nurse Leaders, CNSs, Nursing Professional Development Specialists, and Quality Management Nurses, would be required to attend the first EBP immersion together as a cohort. This ensured all the nursing leadership was learning the method simultaneously, which would mitigate any skepticism and roadblocks to successful EBP adoption. Without leadership engagement and buy-in, the DCNO believed immersion across the enterprise would be futile. Because all nursing leadership was required to participate in the immersion, a safety net was created in the event one level of leadership failed to buy into the enculturation. This unique approach fostered collegial relationships, broke down existing silos, strengthened the department, and built a unique EBP capacity with the goal of preparing all MSK nurses in an established EBP methodology, building EBP competence, and making evidence-based decision-making the standard practice across the nursing enterprise.

Additional deliberate strategies were required to ensure the adoption of EBP at MSK. Recognizing Clinical Nurse Specialists as EBP experts and early adopters, structural changes were necessary to actualize the full vision. In January 2017, the CNS reporting structure was centralized to strengthen, support, and sustain a spirit and culture of inquiry across the care continuum. The vision for EBP enculturation included a call to validate existing policies, procedures, and standards of care and challenge the "Memorial Way" to ensure the existing nursing practice was up to date and in alignment with the evidence and best practice. Collaboration with the well-established and expert team from the Fuld Institute was pivotal to bringing EBP structures and processes to every chairside, bedside, and tableside across the care continuum.

The EBP immersions consisted of a standard curriculum provided by the EBP Institute's faculty and facilitation of implementation by Fuld expert mentors. Multiple cohorts attended the immersion program, with each subsequent cohort strategically assembled to move EBP expertise beyond the leadership cadre by thoughtfully including academic and alliance partners, staff nurses, and interdisciplinary colleagues. All participants were assigned to one of three unique learning tracks in the program: mentor, leader, or academic. Post immersion, each cohort met with a Fuld EBP expert for follow-up and boosters every three months for 15 months. These sessions were focused on feedback, direction, and support. During this same time, the adoption of EBP terminology and methods were introduced across the department and incorporated into shared governance bylaws and promotional and staff development processes. MSK Librarians developed resources for writing PICO questions and offered courses on evidence searching and reference management. Cohort groups presented their 15-month-long work at a peer symposium/celebration. EBP initiative presentations included clinical inquiry, PICO questions, critical appraisal of the body of evidence conducted, synthesis tables, and evidence-based recommendations for practice or administrative changes to be implemented. Many recommendations have been fully implemented and sustained, and whenever appropriate, measurements of clinical outcomes, value, and returns on investments have been reported.

The strategy of leadership engagement first promoted the enculturation of EBP institution-wide and led to measurable outcomes on challenging clinical/institutional initiatives such as falls, handoff, mindfulness, inpatient discharge, palliative care, opioid addiction in the oncology patient, extravasations, etc. To date, more than 60 EBP initiatives have emerged. A measured increase in knowledge of EBP was appreciated because of the intensive immersion. Surveys of knowledge and skill acquisition and attitude about EBP demonstrated a significant change from baseline. A second, unpredicted outcome was that the immersion sparked interest from participants in returning to advanced degree programs.

MSK nursing leadership now utilizes a systematic process for translating evidence into practice. Capitalizing on this new skill set has led to confirmation of existing best practice/policy as well as to bringing novel EBP interventions forward to address universal, ongoing, and problematic clinical issues. The initial leadership immersion became the foundation for embedding EBP into the culture of MSK. Leadership has demonstrated a sustained commitment to the EBP process as mentors, facilitators, and advocates, ultimately impacting patient care in such a positive and meaningful way.

What do you think are the most important leadership actions in this exemplar?

RESPONSE TO THE NARRATIVE

The senior leaders in the organization made a solid commitment to transform the nursing enterprise to an evidence-based approach to decision-making. They collaborated with a well-established external organization with extensive expertise in EBP that was qualified to bring EBP methodology effectively into the organization. They were clear in their communications to all the leaders in the organization about expectation for leaders in this journey. They role modeled the attitude and behaviors they expected from others by attending the education and skill-building program alongside their leadership colleagues and integrating evidence into their own decision-making. They proactively and clearly identified that clinical nurse specialists (CNSs) would be the primary "owners" of EBP in day-to-day practice in their organization and made sure that all the CNSs were educated in the EBP methodology. They reorganized the CNSs into a centralized department with direct report to a single leader and added EBP deliverables to the CNS job description, again, clearly articulating expectations. They promoted uptake and full integration of EBP by aligning this approach with their existing strengths, such as their well-established shared governance program. They developed internal infrastructures and programs to ensure integration and sustainability of EBP methodology across and throughout the entire nursing enterprise, such as the library resources and the educational programs. They celebrated successes and provided appreciation to the EBP teams at ongoing recognition events.

REFLECTIVE QUESTIONS

1. Describe how a partnership with the Helene Fuld Health Trust National Institute for Evidence-based Practice (EBP) impacted the success of the MSK EBP journey.

    Answer: The partnership with the Helene Fuld Health Trust National Institute for Evidence-based Practice (EBP) was put in motion to leverage an innovative, deliberate, and customized college level, deep-dive, five-day EBP immersion for the nursing enterprise at MSK to build EBP competence and establish a singular EBP methodology that would be utilized across the nursing enterprise. This unique approach fostered collegial relationships, broke down existing silos, strengthened the department, and built EBP capacity to make evidence-based decision-making the standard practice across the nursing enterprise.

2. Why was engaging all MSK's nursing leaders as the first EBP cohort so critical to MSK's success?

    Answer: The initial leadership immersion became the foundation for the enculturation of EBP institution-wide, embedded EBP into the operations of MSK, and promoted leaders' sustained commitment to the EBP process as mentors, facilitators, and advocates. The strategy of leadership engagement first has led to measurable outcomes on challenging clinical/institutional initiatives and improved care and outcomes for patients.

3. What are some key leadership strategies that have sustained EBP at MSK?

    Answer:

    - Proactively determining that CNSs would lead EBP work at MSK, moving the CNSs into a centralized department, revising the CNS job description to include EBP work and deliverables, and creating a lead CNS position to oversee the CNS EBP work.

    - Leveraging existing strengths by aligning and integrating EBP work with strong, well-established programs at MSK including the shared governance program, the clinical advancement program, and the staff development program.

    - Engaging the Fuld Institute in conducting follow-up sessions to keep teams on track, reinforce knowledge and skills attained, and provide ongoing support, encouragement, and feedback. These sessions promoted sustained commitment to the projects.

    - Support of internal programs, developed and delivered by MSK mentors, to continue to build EBP capacity and commitment in the organization (education sessions, library resources, policies, and procedures).

4. List three important outcomes that can be actualized when nurse leaders take a systematic approach to developing an evidence-based approach to care.

    Answer:

    - Improved patient outcomes

    - Elevating the profile of nursing within an organization as EBP experts

    - Development of collegial relationships and teamwork among the leadership team

QUIZ QUESTIONS

1. Name the four domains of the use of evidence.

    Answer: Research, Evidence-Based Practice, Process Improvement, and Innovation

2. What is the difference between research and evidence-based practice (EBP)?

    Answer: Research is a rigorous, scholarly process of generating new knowledge or evidence. Evidence-based practice, simply stated, is the application or translation of evidence into practice.

3. Despite a multitude of studies demonstrating that its use leads to quality, safe patient care, which of the four domains is still not hardwired and used throughout operations in healthcare and why?

    Answer: Evidence-Based Practice (EBP) for a multitude of reasons such as lack of leadership support, insufficient time to engage in this process, inability to access data or databases necessary to engage in EBP, lack of mentors or sponsors for such activities.

4. Who is critical for the integration and sustainability of EBP?

   Answer: (Nurse) Leaders at all levels of the organization. At the unit level, nurse managers are critical to enable EBP.

5. How can clinicians be supported to use /apply evidence in their daily practice?

   Answer: When nurse managers create a "spirit of inquiry" and do other things that serve to build an infrastructure to support EBP, clinicians can engage in EBP in the clinical setting. Nurse managers who "model the way" of using evidence in their own practice set the stage for others to do so in their practice. When staff are supported with expert mentors who can guide them in the use of EBP in their practice, they are more successful in doing so. (This answer can vary as there are many examples on "how" in the chapter.)

6. For an organization to be successful in integrating the continuum of best practices and processes to deliver outcomes, what two things must be in place?

   Answer: The organization's culture and readiness to support EBP must be established.

7. What are the three broad categories that characterize the role of the nurse leader to promote the use of EBP by clinicians in their daily practice?

   a) Leading the way for EBP, building an infrastructure for EBP, managing the process for EBP

   b) Building an infrastructure for EBP, determining readiness for EBP, promoting EBP

   c) Leading EBP, building infrastructure for EBP, promoting EBP

   Correct Answer: c

8. Name one organizational model that focuses on the systemwide process for implementation for EBP discussed in this chapter.

   Answer: ARCC Model or i-PARIHS

9. Name one practice change model used to implement EBP discussed in this chapter.

   Answer: Seven Steps of EBP (Melnyk) or Iowa Model for EBP or Johns Hopkins Model for EBP

10. Which is correct regarding the implications for the consistent use of evidence in making clinician decisions/actions?

    a) Only when the use of evidence is the standard of practice will the Quadruple Aim in health be achieved

    b) Nurse leaders who achieve competency in EBP will make effective decisions that can result in achieving targeted outcomes

    c) Leaders who use EBP create future leaders who will use EBP

    d) All the above

    Correct Answer: c

17

WISDOM LEADERSHIP: A DEVELOPMENTAL JOURNEY

REFLECTIVE QUESTIONS

1. What did you appreciate about the discussion of wisdom leadership presented in this chapter?

    Answer: Students identify what they appreciate about wisdom leadership.

2. How did ideas and material presented influence your thinking and feeling?

    Answer: Students identify the ideas and materials from the chapter and explain how they influenced their thinking and feeling.

3. What if any commitments to action will you make because of reading this chapter?

    Answer: Students identify changes in their behavior in light of what they learned from the chapter.

4. How might you apply the Balance Theory of Wisdom to a leadership issue you are currently trying to influence and manage?

    Answer: Student relate the Balance Theory of Wisdom to a leadership issue they are facing in their practice. Through the application of balance theory, the students should identify ways to influence and manage the issue.

5. What aspects of the Balance Theory of Wisdom definition are you dealing with successfully? What needs more attention?

    Answer: Students identify aspects of the balance theory definition they are dealing with successfully and what needs more attention.

6. As you reflect on the adult cognitive developmental stages presented in this work, what is your personal assessment of your current stage of development?

    Answer: Students identify their current stage of development based on the cognitive development stages presented in the chapter.

7. In your own words, how do you explain the differences between horizontal and vertical leadership development?

    Answer: In their own words, students state the difference between horizontal and vertical leadership.

8. Read and reflect on Nic Petrie's 2015 article, "The How to of Vertical Leadership Development" https://www.ccl.org/wp-content/uploads/2015/04/verticalLeadersPart2.pdf

    Which of the 15 approaches Petrie suggests are of interest to you and relevant to your leadership development plans?

    Answer: Students identify which of the 15 approaches are of interest to them and relevant to their leadership development plans.

9. What are strategies one can use to teach wisdom or develop wisdom capacities with students, peers, and/ or colleagues?

    Answer: Students identify strategies they can creatively use to teach and develop wisdom leaders.

NARRATIVE

Note to facilitator(s): The author of this chapter chose to incorporate and thread their narrative throughout the chapter. Please refer students to the textbook chapter for discussion.

QUIZ QUESTIONS

1. Wisdom capacities include the ability to reflect, forgive, and be humble, trustworthy, compassionate, relationship-oriented, and positive.

    a) True

    b) False

    Correct Answer: a

2.   Wisdom capacities include the ability to problem solve and get to a right answer given a challenge or issue to solve.

      a) True

      b) False

Correct Answer: b

Rationale: Wisdom capacities include the ability to appreciate and apply systems thinking and derive meaning from the analysis and evaluation of competing values and complexity dynamics.

3.   Wise leaders ask different questions, seek multiple perspectives, and see and think in systems.

      a) True

      b) False

Correct Answer: a

4.   The action logic of impulsivity can be classified at what stage of adult cognitive development?

      a) Preconventional

      b) Conventional

      c) Post-conventional

Correct Answer: a

5.   The action logic of strategist can be classified at what stage of adult cognitive development?

      a) Preconventional

      b) Conventional

      c) Post-conventional

Correct Answer: c

6.   A wise person has learned to balance three aspects of behavior: cognition, affect, and volition.

      a) True

      b) False

Correct Answer: a

7.   Researchers Joiner and Josephs (2006) argue wise and successful leaders master four types of agility related to:

      a) Vision, mission, goals, and strategic plans

      b) Self, context, stakeholders, and creativity

      c) Creating, competing, controlling, and collaborating

      d) Budgets, financial planning, investments, and resource management

Correct Answer: b

8. Horizontal leadership development helps people acquire more intricate and advanced ways of thinking and perspective taking.

    a) True

    b) False

Correct Answer: b

Rationale: Horizontal leadership involves the acquisition and use of information (e.g., data analytics), skills (e.g., conflict resolution), and competencies (e.g., strategic planning techniques) essential for performance.

9. According to Angela Barron McBride there are five stages to a career. The stages are:

    a) Initiating, Development, Collaboration, Cooperation, Independence

    b) Novice, Advanced Beginner, Competent, Proficient, Expert

    c) Preparation, Independent Contributions, Development of Home Setting, Development of the Field, the Gadfly Wise Person Period

    d) Noticing, Reflecting, Interpreting, Responding, Evaluating

Correct Answer: c

10. The Teaching Wisdom Project suggests which of the following procedures to support the teaching of wisdom:

    a) Encourage students to read classic works and reflect on the wisdom of the sages.

    b) Engage students in discussion about what they have read and how lessons learned can be applied in their own lives.

    c) Challenge students to think about their own values and how their values influence their thinking and reasoning.

    d) Encourage students to consider the role of critical, creative, and practical thinking when confronted with challenges and dilemmas.

    e) Encourage students to weigh the good and bad outcomes of a course of action with a greater good in mind.

    f) Teachers should role model wise thinking for students as they propose problems raise questions and tackle complex dilemmas and situations.

    g) All the above

Correct Answer: g

18

DIVERSITY, EQUITY, AND INCLUSION IN EDUCATION AND HEALTH SYSTEMS

REFLECTIVE QUESTIONS

1. Name one way in which racism, discrimination, and inequity reflect in nursing.

    Answer: Nursing's inability to recruit and retain students who identify as Black, Indigenous, and other people of color

2. How can we create safe academic environments to recruit and retain American Indian and other students of color into graduate nursing programs to diversify nursing leadership roles?

    Answer:

    -   Refrain from the notion of "colorblindness." This includes beliefs such as "treating everyone the same," or the avoidance of challenging dialogue around issues of history, race, oppression, and politics.

    -   Resist the assumption that all American Indian students represent or are intimately knowledgeable about their ancestry and culture. Due to assimilation and termination policies, many American Indians did not grow up on their reservations or were not raised with traditional ways of being and knowing. Some students can feel confused or ashamed of this.

    -   Ask students what we can do as faculty to support them in their learning.

3. How can we remove barriers to promotion and tenure for American Indian and other scholars of color within academic institutions?

   Answer:
   - Resist tokenizing American Indian and other faculty of color, particularly to satisfy "diversity requirements."

   - Prioritize the inclusion of faculty of color within research and writing groups to provide a supportive environment.

   - Evaluate promotion policies and requirements to ensure that they are equitable for all scholars and value all areas of research and consider whether diverse scholars are being recognized for their work within their communities.

4. How do you foster an inclusive environment for patients and nurses of color in your unit, and what is the role of nurse leaders in promoting inclusive environments?

   Answer: Leadership support and commitment to diversity, equity, and inclusion (DEI) is important for promoting an environment that is safe for all. Adoption and reinforcement of policies that address discriminatory practices will provide guidance for the team. As leaders you will also be responsible for providing resources to victims who have experienced any form of discrimination. It is also important to stand up for victims and to advocate that administration follows through with such incidents. Create a nurturing environment that allows open communication and feedback and be proactive in addressing any concerns. Promote fairness in the workplace and ensure that all your staff have equal opportunities for professional growth. Lastly, as global leaders, set a good example for others in your team and across the globe by speaking up and collaborating with other institutions on how to push forward the work on DEI.

5. What is the role of administrative leaders in nursing higher education to engage in racial justice and equity work?

   Answer: To question systems of power that disadvantage Black, Indigenous, and people of color (BIPOC) individuals and groups; promote policies that prioritize equity and inclusion for all, not just the majority; and self-reflect and question White dominant systems and traditions within schools of nursing.

NARRATIVE

Rachel is a registered nurse on a medical-surgical unit who identifies as African American/Black. At the beginning of her shift Rachel is assigned to a 55-year-old White male patient. During her routine assessments, the patient asked if Rachel could call the nurse to the room. Rachel explained that she is a registered nurse, and she has the necessary training to manage the patient's condition. The patient became upset and asked Rachel to call her supervisor.

You are a nurse manager on a medical-surgical unit. When you enter the room, the patient says: "I do not want a Black nurse. I would prefer to have a White nurse. I am not sure if she knows what she is doing." Rachel also verbalizes to you that she feels discriminated against based on her race despite her competence to carry out the assigned tasks.

How do you respond to this encounter?

1. Describe ways you can assess this situation as part of the de-escalation process.

2. What are the ethical implications that should be considered in this scenario?

3. Discuss the process for documenting patient's refusal of treatment.

4. What are some effective ways an institution can promote inclusion and recognition for nurses of color on your unit?

5. List some of the implications that this encounter would have on Rachel and other nurses of color.

RESPONSE TO THE NARRATIVE

Assess the situation and observe for discomfort in both the patient and Rachel. Acknowledge Rachel's concerns about the situation being discriminatory and explain that you value the contribution that she brings to the team. State that Rachel is a qualified registered nurse and has the knowledge and skills to manage the patient's condition, and we do not switch out care providers based on race, religion, gender, sexual orientation, or national origin. If non-discriminatory policies are available in your hospital, review with the patient that discriminatory requests are not accommodated in the institution. If the patient continues to insist on a change of care, document their refusal of care and offer to help them with a transfer to another facility. Debrief with Rachel about the situation; offer recognition of her efforts and contribution to the team. Call the Employee Assistance Program (EAP) or other support for Rachel as she deals with this situation.

QUIZ QUESTIONS

1. What are the sources of discrimination for BIPOC nurses on inpatient units?

   a) Patients

   b) Staff

   c) Nurse leaders

   d) All the above

   Correct Answer: d

2. Select the concepts that are important for leaders of nursing schools to understand (select all that apply): _____.

   a) Intersectionality

   b) Decolonizing perspectives

   c) Anti-racist pedagogy

   d) White privilege and diversity

   e) All the above

   Correct Answer: e

3. Administrators and faculty in schools of nursing currently must demonstrate a baseline level of competency to engage in conversations about diversity.

      a) True

      b) False

Correct Answer: b

4. Is it OK to assume that an American Indian graduate student in your class can speak on behalf of all American Indians about a particular topic that is being discussed in class?

      a) Yes

      b) No

Correct Answer: b

5. Select the concept(s) that are important for leaders of nursing schools to avoid when trying to create a safe environment for BIPOC faculty (select all that apply): _____.

      a) Resisting colorblindness

      b) Tokenizing BIPOC faculty

      c) Incorporating land acknowledgements into campus policies and procedures

      d) Indigenizing curriculum

Correct Answer: b

6. Discrimination towards BIPOC patients can result in long-term health consequences.

      a) True

      b) False

Correct Answer: a

7. What is the best response to a patient who requests to switch their provider from a BIPOC nurse to a White nurse?

      a) Respect patient's rights and switch provider

      b) Decline patient's request and offer transfer if necessary

      c) Have a White and BIPOC nurse share responsibility for the client

      d) All the above

Correct Answer: b

8. Reflexivity on the part of faculty is valuable to enhancing faculty understanding of their social location in relation to their students and determining how best to create a more nurturing environment that facilitates student success.

      a) True

      b) False

Correct Answer: a

9. Academic climate is one of the most important factors for the academic success of BIPOC students.

    a) True

    b) False

    Correct Answer: a

10. Intervention(s) that support the success of BIPOC students in nursing academia include: _____.

    a) Listening sessions

    b) Creating safe spaces

    c) Fostering trusting relationships between BIPOC students and faculty

    d) All the above

    Correct Answer: d

19

TRANSFORMING HEALTH POLICY

REFLECTIVE QUESTIONS

1. Briefly describe the five-phase model of policymaking.

   Answer: Policymaking begins with agenda-setting or bringing issues/problems to the attention of policymakers. Second, potential policies are considered, and consideration is given to the costs and benefits of the policies as well as the perspectives of stakeholders, the media, interest groups, and influential individuals. Third, how decisions are made largely depends on the legislative system of the country. Still, a process is undertaken to determine whether or not the potential policy will be accepted or passed. Fourth, the policy is implemented, and again the process is largely determined by that nation's political culture. Finally, policy evaluation includes determining if a policy met its projected goals, what unintended consequences there may be, and if it could be modified to be more effective. Sometimes a return to the agenda-setting step in the cycle is indicated.

2. How can nurses play a role in each of the five phases of policymaking?

   Answer: Nurses as collective groups can bring up issues, and nursing professional organizations do this particularly well. At the policy formation stage, nursing interest groups may ask individual members to contact their elected officials to help support or oppose a particular policy. During the decision-making process, nursing groups may support policy by persuasion (e.g., asking individuals to write letters, op-eds, make calls, etc.), but also persuade at a group level using political action committee (PAC) funding for that organization to support candidates. During policy implementation, nursing organizations can choose individual nurse experts to inform them and/or speak together about the policy implementation process. Finally, individual nurse scientists can evaluate the impact of policies on health outcomes. Nursing organizations can fund, cite, and support that evaluation work and advance it.

3. Describe policy-related activities that nurses can engage in at the individual level.

    Answer: Nurses can talk with policymakers as experts in quality, safety, and the patient experience. They can use their positional power as nurses and their expert power as those closest to patients. They can also use their individual and collective persuasion power in various stages of the policymaking process. Nurses are uniquely positioned all over the world to argue for healthcare as a human right. Nurse scientists can contribute to the evidence and critically appraise who and what is missing from the evidence.

4. How do nursing professional organizations participate in the policymaking process?

    Answer: Nursing professional organizations can exert influence in all five phases of the policymaking process. They can raise issues with legislators, hire professionals to help formulate policy, have expert members serve on rule writing committees on behalf of nursing, and connect their members with professional policymakers and lobbyists to learn skills, comment on policy implementation, sponsor analysis of the impact of policies on outcomes, and be the loud and strong voice of a large portion of the workforce and a trusted profession.

5. Name and reflect on sources of power that you possess that you may not have been aware of previously.

    Answer: Nurses really are experts in quality, safety, and the patient experience, and they rarely see themselves that way. As one of the least trusted professions in the US, politicians want to be advised by nurses (one of the most trusted professions in the US) and make those critical connections. Nurses are also skilled in persuasion and advocacy. Nurses can speak to healthcare as a human right, contribute to the evidence, and critically appraise existing evidence in addition to what is missing.

NARRATIVE

Nurse and patient advocacy groups in North Carolina (NC) have been calling for the removal of physician supervisory requirements for NC's advanced practice registered nurses (APRNs). NC law currently requires APRNs to have a collaborative practice agreement with a supervising physician. These physicians do not actually "supervise" or even work in the same location as the APRN, and, in many cases, APRNs must pay physicians to serve as their supervisors. NC is one of only a handful of states that continues to require collaborative practice agreements. APRN education and certification have been standardized nationally since the early 1990s, and research indicates APRNs provide safe, effective care. Research also indicates collaborative practice/supervisory requirements increase the cost of care, decrease access to care, and provide no value to patient care. Yet NC, a rural state where millions of citizens experience significant disparities in healthcare access, continues to restrict the APRN practice.

The NC SAVE Act (NC Senate Bill 249/House Bill 277) would remove physician oversight requirements for NC's APRNs. NC State Representative Gale Adcock, who is a nurse practitioner, introduced the SAVE Act to NC's legislature in the 2021 session. The bill has bipartisan support and is also sponsored by the other three registered nurses who serve in NC's legislature, among other legislative members. Groups supporting the legislation include the North Carolina Nurses Association and its PAC, the AARP North Carolina, Americans for Prosperity North Carolina, the March of Dimes, the National Academy of Medicine, and the Rural Center. Business groups including the Convenient Care Association and Amazon also endorse the bill, citing its potential for improving access to healthcare. Only physician groups oppose the legislation, citing unsubstantiated patient safety concerns.

The NC legislature has considered bills related to APRN supervision several times over the past few years. In past sessions, bills that would have removed APRN practice restrictions died during the legislative session. Nurse and patient advocacy groups hope the bill will be passed this session. The SAVE Act has the bipartisan support of a record number of NC Representatives and Senators. The COVID-19 crisis highlighted the fragility of the state's healthcare system and the importance of increasing healthcare access, particularly in NC's rural regions. Moreover, as part of efforts to increase healthcare access during the COVID-19 crisis, the NC legislature temporarily lifted several restrictions on APRN practice that would be made permanent if the SAVE Act is passed. Lifting these APRN practice restrictions may have illustrated to lawmakers that the restrictions served no purpose but to restrict healthcare access.

1. How do you think nurses, both individually and collectively, helped get the issue of physician oversight of APRNs on the policy agenda? How might their framing of the issue have garnered widespread support?

2. Who are the stakeholders in this legislation, and what do you imagine their concerns are?

3. What can nurses do, both individually and collectively, to encourage members of the NC legislature to vote in favor of the bill?

4. What role do PACs play? What role do lobbyists play? How could theories about agenda setting help us understand what forces might contribute to the bill's success this session?

RESPONSE TO THE NARRATIVE

Individual nurses, nursing professional organizations, and patient advocacy groups worked to get APRN supervision on the policy agenda. Important to garnering broad legislative and public support, supervisory requirements were framed as an obstacle to accessible and affordable healthcare. Since NC is one of only a handful of states with such physician supervisory requirements, nurse groups could cite research linking removing supervisory access to decreased healthcare costs and increased healthcare access and assure the public that removing these barriers would not compromise patient safety or quality of care.

North Carolina nurses and nurse groups received support from patient advocacy groups such as the AARP and the March of Dimes. These groups partnered with national nursing organizations such as the ANA and the AANP to move the agenda forward.

The North Carolina Nurses Association (NCNA) was empowered by its membership to advocate for this legislation. Member dues support public education campaigns and lobbying activities. NCNA lobbyists directly attempt to persuade legislators to vote in favor of the legislation and educate nurse members on how to effectively pressure their representatives to vote for the legislation. The association's political action committee (PAC) supported candidates who expressed that they would vote in favor of the legislation. The election of four registered nurses who supported the bill also helped the bill gain increasing support.

Individual nurses supported this legislation by contacting their legislators, writing letters to the editors, and participating in advocacy activities organized by the NCNA, including Nurses Day at the Legislature and special meetings called to consider the SAVE Act. Individual nurses provided powerful stories about how current laws constrained their ability to provide care, particularly in NC's many rural regions. Their stories emphasized how current legislation exacerbates healthcare disparities experienced by North Carolinians.

Finally, COVID-19 underscored the dearth of healthcare providers in NC's rural regions and the importance of removing regulatory barriers. In essence, the pandemic created the window of opportunity described by Kingdon's Three Streams Theory. Nurse groups advocated for the temporary removal of critical elements of physician oversight to facilitate access to care during the pandemic. Nurse groups can now point to the results of easing of these restrictions: increased access to care without decreased quality of care, evidence of the superfluous nature of NC's APRN practice restrictions.

QUIZ QUESTIONS

1. All the following are stages of the policy process except:

   a) Agenda setting

   b) Policy formulation

   c) Decision-making

   d) Policy implementation

   e) The PDSA cycle

   Correct Answer: e

2. Which of the following are in Kingdon's Multiple Streams Theory related to agenda-setting?

   a) Problems or issues

   b) Solutions or policies

   c) Political conditions

   d) All the above

   e) None of the above

   Correct Answer: d

3. A country's political system determines nurses' access to the policymaking process.

   a) True

   b) False

   Correct Answer: a

4. The American Nurses Association comments on draft rules and regulations.

   a) True

   b) False

   Correct Answer: a

5. The terms used when one individual/group has special information that another person/group wants is:

   a) Collective power

   b) Bargaining power

   c) Information power

   d) Coercive power

   e) Positional power

   Correct Answer: c

6. The concept of healthcare as a human right can be used to challenge policies that compromise a human's right to healthcare.

   a) True

   b) False

   Correct Answer: a

7. International non-governmental organizations (INGOs) can engage in political advocacy and national policy processes on behalf of donors.

   a) True

   b) False

   Correct Answer: a

8. Advocating for equity and social justice in resource allocation, access to healthcare, and other social and economic services falls outside the scope of nursing.

   a) True

   b) False

   Correct Answer: b

9. All the following are federal legislative priorities of the American Nurses Association except:

   a) Safe staffing

   b) COVID-19

   c) Minimizing violence in the workplace

   d) Reducing CAUTI and CLABSI rates

   e) Health system transformation

   Correct Answer: d

10. Professional nursing organizations carry out which of the following functions:

    a) Organizing nurses into unions

    b) Providing a voice of nursing to legislators

    c) Educating nurses about advocacy

    d) Both b & c

    e) None of the above

    Correct Answer: d

20

LEADERSHIP IN SOCIAL AND POLITICAL DETERMINANTS OF HEALTH

REFLECTIVE QUESTIONS

1. Review the CDC website on Social Determinants of Health: https://www.cdc.gov/socialdeterminants/index.htm

   What SDOH effects have you seen regularly in your professional role? What are some current federal, state, or local healthcare policies that might address the issue?

   Answer: May include any from the website with broad categories of access to care, education access, social and community context, neighborhood and built environment, economic stability. Students then review federal, state, and/or local policies that would address the issue.

2. Why is it important to address both?

   Answer: Learner should explore how politics and policy influence funding and resources available to address specific SDOH.

3. Why is it important for nurses to infuse loving-kindness as they use Unitary Caring Science approaches in their advocacy work?

   Answer: This helps us to understand and realize our oneness and connection to each other.

4. Reflect on your own structural racism experiences and biases in healthcare that you have experienced or witnessed as a patient, a family member, or a provider. How can we begin to dismantle structural racism?

   Answer: Using critical race theory, acting as political advocates as part of our role as nurses.

5. Create a visual representation of the intersection of SPDH, Unitary Caring Science, and political advocacy. Prepare to discuss this or create a narrative around it. How are political determinants of health different from social determinants of health?

   Answer: This should be a visual, creative work and be original from each student. They should be able to discuss the intersecting areas.

NARRATIVE

A Black 47-year-old man living with heart failure (whom we will call Al) was enrolled in a research study at the local safety-net hospital. Al was hesitant to be involved with his cardiology team, and at enrollment into the research study with the research nurse and social worker, he talked about how he didn't trust healthcare. He shared that a family member of his was experimented on in the Tuskegee airmen experiments. Al felt his family had been experimented on enough throughout their history by healthcare professionals who were supposed to help them.

Al talked about how the historical impact of healthcare's inequitable treatment of minoritized groups like his family had made him so fearful of healthcare that he didn't get help for his severe edema, shortness of breath, and chest pain until he could no longer work because of the severity of his symptoms. He wasn't willing to have his heart failure more actively managed by his cardiology team. Because of his passive response to his illness, he had only ended up accessing care when he was in an emergency state. Al shared that he had joined the research study only to share his experience and wanted to make sure people weren't being experimented on as they had been in the past.

This is an example of how healthcare and policy created situations that exploited minoritized groups and destroyed trust with people who needed to be included and welcomed. This patient's historical experience with systematic oppression was directly impacting his relationship with his healthcare providers in the current day.

1. How would you approach caring for Al using a Unitary Caring Science and/ or critical race theory perspective?

2. Al's cardiology research team could have felt this man was "noncompliant" because he didn't follow up with his appointments or take his prescribed medications. How can you frame his actions from a Unitary Caring Science that examines the SPDH of this situation?

3. How would you share Al's experience with the cardiology research team?

4. What does this example teach us about patients who are given labels like "noncompliant" or "difficult"? Using a critical race theory perspective, what are the underlying social constructs of systemic racism related to these labels and Al's experience?

RESPONSE TO THE NARRATIVE

1. Ways to apply Unitary Caring Science could include: intentionally working to build trust before providing care, listening authentically to Al's story and experience, and intentionally building a transpersonal caring relationship.

   Ways to apply critical race theory could include: examining power structures and historical oppression in Al's story, offering understanding around hesitation to access healthcare due to historical racism, acknowledging the impact of historical racism in health inequity.

2. Application of Unitary Caring Science allows the healthcare provider to see Al's hesitancy to see healthcare providers and to take his medication as prescribed as symptomatic of the healthcare system and structural oppression instead of Al just being "difficult." By acknowledging Al's humanity, the provider is able to meet Al where he is at, acknowledg his experience, and build trust before asking him to do things to manage his health. Establishing this relationship helps to set both Al and his healthcare provider up for a successful treatment relationship.

3. Sharing Al's story with the cardiology research team is important context for the team to understand. Highlighting how his experience with institutional racism and oppression is impacting his healthcare decisions might help the team to understand the importance of building a trusting relationship before jumping to treatment. It could be helpful to work on a small achievable goal at first to build success and trust with the team and Al.

4. Al's story highlights the importance of examining medical labels that are often ascribed to people from minoritized groups. Patients who are labeled as "noncompliant" may be hesitant to follow recommendations from healthcare providers because of past experience or because of distrust in institutions like healthcare and government that have historically oppressed people of color and other minoritized groups.

QUIZ QUESTIONS

1. The concept that all members of society should have the same basic rights, protection, opportunities, and social benefits is called:

   a) Diversity

   b) Equity

   c) Social justice

   d) All the above

   Correct Answer: c

2. What is the difference between equality and equity?

    a) Equality is providing the same resources to everyone, while equity is providing help to only the worst-off communities.

    b) Equality provides needed resources tailored to each group, while equity provides the same resources to everyone.

    c) Equality is providing the same resources to everyone, while equity provides needed resources to each group.

    d) Equality provides resources to only the worst-off communities, while equity provides the same resources to everyone.

    Correct Answer: c

3. How do diversity, equity, and inclusion improve nursing leadership?

    a) Creates trust with a community

    b) Improves the amount of work a team can get done

    c) More accurately represents the population nursing serves

    d) Both a & c

    Correct Answer: d

4. How do diversity, equity, and inclusion improve the nursing discipline?

    a) Creates trust with a community

    b) Improves innovation and diversity of ideas

    c) Both a & b

    d) None of the above

    Correct Answer: b

5. Social determinants of health are independent of stigma.

    a) True

    b) False

    Correct Answer: b

6. A socioeconomically disadvantaged community experiencing pollution from a chemical plant is an example of a political determinant of health.

    a) True

    b) False

    Correct Answer: a

7. How does the historical impact of inequitable policies impact healthcare?

    a) Inequitable policies do not influence healthcare.

    b) There are not historical inequities.

    c) By creating advantages for some groups and not for others, society limits individuals' ability to create healing and health.

    d) All the above

Correct Answer: c

8. Nurses can be very effective advocates and leaders in addressing SPDH because they understand the whole person.

    a) True

    b) False

Correct Answer: a

9. The base of Unitary Caring Science is centered on the nurse's impact on patient care.

    a) True

    b) False

Correct Answer: b

10. The COVID-19 pandemic created health disparities that caused minoritized populations to suffer from more significant adverse health outcomes.

    a) True

    b) False

Correct Answer: a

21

CREATING A CONNECTED WORLD: A CALL TO ETHICS OF FACE AND BELONGING

REFLECTIVE QUESTIONS

1. How does the concept of an inflection point in business inform leaders' decision-making moving forward?

    Answer: The inflection point is a change in the business environment that dramatically shifts some element of your activities, throwing certain taken-for-granted assumptions into question (McGrath, 2019).

2. What role/function do white space, unusual suspects, and serendipity play as aspects of chaos theory?

    Answer: *White space* is a term from publishing describing the white space surrounding a word or letter on a page. The white space is needed to enable the word, writing, or object to be readable or legible on a page. Without white space, words and letters would not be distinguishable from the other words, letters, or objects on the page. Unusual suspects are those individuals who have a stake in a process or outcome that are not usually thought of as having any influence. Usual processes are thought of as routines with usual players or stakeholders. Individuals on the periphery of a process or outcome are not usually included in the decision-making or asked for their input. These individuals view a process or outcome from a different vantage point that often can shed a different perspective on an issue, process, or outcome. Their unique vantage point can be insightful and provocative and often redefines the assumptions. These individuals often see an inflection point before leadership does as they work at the point of care delivery. Serendipity is when seemingly disparate individuals, processes, or outcomes come together to create something new and beneficial for all parties in ways that could not have been foretold or imagined. Serendipity occurs in the space between planning and luck. (Brafman & Pollack, 2013)

3. How might learning "to hold opposites or paradoxical concepts in the same space" help with decision-making in the delivery of healthcare?

   Answer: The concept of "holding paradoxical thoughts in the same space" is called *polarity management* (Manderscheid & Freeman, 2012; Peterson, 2017; Sabetzadeh et al., 2011). Healthcare is protocol and guideline driven; reducing variation is part of the evidence-based practice (EBP) initiative. There are occasions where two opposing concepts need to be held in the same space. The dissonance that is created when these concepts are held within the same space or conversation is where many patients, families, and their loved ones live. Healthcare providers often receive no training on how to manage in this conundrum. Gaining clarity on the issue is key to finding meaning and purpose in this dilemma. Authentic listening is the key to being present to paradoxes.

4. The affective domain is often called the "soft skills" domain. How has the pandemic affected healthcare providers' sense of purpose and meaning with the work they perform? Support your position.

   Answer: The affective domain, often called "soft skills," involves the social aspect of healthcare. It is in the affective domain that meaning and purpose are assigned by the individual in both the work they perform and the relationships that sustain that work. The affective domain is where patients and families register their satisfaction with their expectations of the care they received. The affective domain is where we house our feelings. When healthcare providers talk about the dimension of work where "they don't feel cared for," this takes place in the affective domain. The pain from the last year of this pandemic is working for organizations where providers "didn't feel cared for." The inability to process this stress will affect recruiting, hiring, retention, and the rate of retirements for all sectors of the healthcare industry. Frontline workers will have major mental health issues for some time to come. The mental health of the frontline staff will have major implications for the healthcare industry for years to come, and their mental health will be the 800-pound gorilla in the room for the healthcare recovery trajectory.

5. How do the concepts of white space, unusual suspects, and serendipity support diversity, equity, and inclusion initiatives?

   Answer: Diversity, equity, and inclusion are enhanced by the concepts of white space, unusual suspects, and serendipity. Humans love patterns and routine in their lives. It lends a feeling of security and sense of purpose at work. Pausing or stepping back from an issue to allow the emotions and dust to settle around it gives individuals space to see the contours of the issue in a new light; that pause interrupts the normal patterns and allows space for new patterns or elements to emerge from the shadows. Unusual suspects force the issue of stakeholders and community of interest to think of who is *not* at the table that might have information, influence, or be part of the decision-making process who is normally not invited. Thoughts from the fringe can be the weak signals detected by the inflection point processes. Serendipity is a mindset that allows for new connections and relationships to be forged and solidified. Serendipity allows for mystery to unfold. It is not planned for nor calculated but witnessed and appreciated.

NARRATIVE

A large, vertically integrated health system with a Unitary Caring Science (UCS) affiliation identified a business need to increase the number of BSN-prepared nurses within their organization as part of the journey toward Magnet status. After conducting a review of the nursing workforce, the organization realized that their nursing workforce had a retention rate that remained relatively constant over the study period. Given that these nurses would remain with the organization until retirement, replacing them with BSN-prepared nurses was not going to accomplish the 80% target goal for the Magnet journey during their projected timeline. The organization had a longstanding academic-service partnership with a private local health sciences university. A proposal to create an RN-to-BSN program with a UCS foundation was made to this university. The proposal included significant tuition support for working nurses who wished to return to school to complete this degree. The program's stated ultimate objective was to change the nursing culture at this organization.

How can the six human attributes of the 21st century Conceptual Age be integrated into both the educational and practice settings of these organizations to engage and ultimately retain nurses in the organization and/or profession?

RESPONSE TO THE NARRATIVE

Academic-service partnerships are a path forward to assist moving organizations from VUCA to VUCA 2.0; Volatility to Vision, Uncertainty to Understanding, Complexity to Clarity, and Ambiguity to Agility (Yoder-Wise, 2021). The old medical industrialized model of healthcare delivery is at inflection points across sectors, requiring a reimagining of what skill sets will be required as those assumptions no longer apply. Elevation of the affective domain skill sets (heart-centered) will be required as many of the cognitive (head-centered) and psychomotor (hand-centered) skills will be transformed by machine learning and interface with patients and families. An essential skill will be to navigate the whitewater of emotions and "being present" during paradoxes and polarities that arise. Academic-service partnerships can serve as incubators for this type of innovation.

Yoder-Wise, P. S. (2021). From VUCA to VUCA 2.0: Surviving today to prosper tomorrow. *Nurs Educ Perspect, 42*(1), 1–2. https://doi.org/10.1097/01.NEP.0000000000000774

QUIZ QUESTIONS

1. An inflection point, in a business context, is about gathering signals of business model assumptions from the edges of the interactions with clients where assumptions might be challenged.

    a) True

    b) False

    Correct Answer: a

2. The utilization of white space, as applied in the business context, is about testing the assumptions of the original business model to the weak signals found at the edges of the current business delivery.

     a) True

     b) False

Correct Answer: a

3. Utilization of the "unusual suspects" part of chaos theory is about looking for those current stakeholders who are *not* usually included in decision-making in a given work unit.

     a) True

     b) False

Correct Answer: a

4. Utilization of diversity, equity, and inclusion (DEI) is about inviting those who are not accustomed to being part of a decision-making role into that process.

     a) True

     b) False

Correct Answer: a

5. Polarity management is about creating space to hold two disparate concepts in the same cognitive decision-making space.

     a) True

     b) False

Correct Answer: a

6. The six human attributes required of the Conceptual Age include:

     a) Design, Work, Story, Caring, Play, Meaning

     b) Design, Work, Story, Empathy, Play, Meaning

     c) Symphony, Design, Story, Empathy, Play, Meaning

     d) Symphony, Work, Empathy, Story, Play, Meaning

     e) Meaning, Play, Caring, Story, Design, Symphony

Correct Answer: c

7. Social determinants of health are non-medical factors that contribute to the health and well-being of an individual.

     a) True

     b) False

Correct Answer: a

8. The experience of discrimination is not considered a social determinant of health.

    a) True

    b) False

    Correct Answer: b

    Rationale: All forms of discrimination, including racism and implicit bias, can be considered SDOH.

9. Levinasian Ethics supports that in order to be, one must be gainfully employed.

    a) True

    b) False

    Correct Answer: b

    Rationale: Levinasian ethics support that in order to be, one must belong.

10. Screening patients for SDOH is an upstream tactic employed to promote health.

    a) True

    b) False

    Correct Answer: b

    Rationale: The screening of patients for SDOH is a midstream tactic.

11. The provision of direct care to patients is a downstream tactic.

    a) True

    b) False

    Correct Answer: a

12. Upstream tactics to promote health include the enactment of laws and regulations that have a broad impact on community well-being.

    a) True

    b) False

    Correct Answer: a